How to Select
The Best Psychological Theory
to be an Effective Counselor
to your Clients:

An Introduction
to Vision Counseling

How to Select
The Best Psychological Theory
to be an Effective Counselor
to your Clients:

An Introduction
to Vision Counseling

J.J. McMahon
P.D., Ph. D.

Studies in Health and Human Services
Volume 15

The Edwin Mellen Press
Lewiston●Queenston●Lampeter

Library of Congress Cataloging-in-Publication Data

McMahon, Joseph.
　　How to select the best psychological theory to be an effective counselor to your clients / Joseph McMahon.
　　　　p. cm. -- (Studies in health and human services ; v. 15)
　　ISBN 0-88946-004-3
　　1. Counselor and client--Philosophy. 2. Counselor and client-- Methodology. 3. Counseling--Philosophy. 4. Counseling--Methodology. 5. Psychology--Philosophy. I. Title. II. Series.
BF637.C6M38 1988
158'.3--dc19　　　　　　　　　　　　　　　　　　　88-12266
　　　　　　　　　　　　　　　　　　　　　　　　　　CIP

This is volume 15 in the continuing series
Studies in Health & Human Services
Volume 15 ISBN 0-88946-004-3
SHHS Series ISBN 0-88946-126-0

For information contact: The Edwin Mellen Press

Box 450　　　　　　　　　　　　　　　　Box 67
Lewiston, New York　　　　　　　Queenston, Ontario
USA 14092　　　　　　　　　　　　L0S 1L0 CANADA
　　　　　　　　Mellen House
　　　　　Lampeter, Dyfed, Wales
　　　UNITED KINGDOM SA48 7DY

Printed in the United States of America

To My Friends and Colleagues
who are a reservoir of
Encouragement and Inspiration

TABLE OF CONTENTS

How to Select
The Best Psychological Theory
to be an Effective Counselor
to your Clients:

An Introduction
to Vision Counseling

Part One

Theory and Skills of Helping

Chapter I

VISION AND THEORIES OF COUNSELING

A Note on Vision

The content of the book flows from the idea that helping people means to cooperate with them in realizing their vision of themselves. The book shows how people's downward movement toward self-destruction and upward movement toward making their world are connected to their ways of thinking and their philosophy of life. The following Human Tendencies Profile, a novel approach to helping, is a map showing the paths to tragedy, survival and creation.

Human Tendencies Profile

Irrational	Rational	Supra-Rational
confusion	order	vision
dependence	control	freedom
rebellion	system	change
skepticism	certainty	creativity
(move down toward)	(move toward)	(move up toward)
self-destruction	self-profit	making our world

Most of us that have had extensive experience in education and the helping professions know about the intellectual poverty cutting across all groups in the American population. Whether we are mentally above average, average or below average, we all need the same intellectual nourishment to make a worthwhile life. In the last thirty years we have taught people how to function well. They can more than meet their economic needs. However, we have failed in helping the new generation to develop their vision of life. We have *trained* them well.

1

They are long on using techniques reflexively and short on thinking reflectively. As educators and psychotherapists we know from experience that many people today are inept at thinking their way through the paradoxes of life. Without a vision that is articulated in an ever expanding philosophy of life, the paradoxes of living will tie us up in psychological knots.

Helping people is difficult. Helping people close to us can be even more difficult. In this note I want to share with you my conviction about helping people either in a professional or nonprofessional way. That conviction is that helping people in the broadest and deepest sense means to cooperate with them in discovering and developing their spiritual powers of intuition, self-reflection, choice and creativity, so that they will have both a clear vision of their lives and the "know-how" to live out that vision. Helping people is like helping the hungry person. We can give him a loaf of bread or we can teach him how to farm, so that he can grow his own grain and make his own bread. We have two problems with the long range solution of teaching a person how to farm. The two problems are the helper and the helpee. Both want immediate satisfaction. The helpee wants to eat now, and the helper wants the immediate gratification of solving the problem on the spot. However, our common sense tells us that we have truly helped people if they become intellectually independent and resourceful.

This book is about helping people make their world according to their vision of life. Cooperating with people to develop a vision of life means to dialogue with them so that they use their powers of intuition, self-reflection, choice and creativity. To develop vision means to carry on a internal dialogue between what is ultimately important to us and how that important reality will guide our thoughts and actions in the present moment. When we dialogue we are developing a philosophy of life, that is, we are nurturing a growing system of ideas that inspires us and guides us toward productive action. Without a living philosophy of life nurtured by our best intuitions we will feel psychologically weak. Gordon Allport, the noted psychologist of personality theory, pointed out that a philosophy of life is necessary for the development of a healthy personality. However, no one can give another person a vision of life. We can help another person to construct his vision by dialoguing with him, but in the end vision is the result of reflecting on one's own intuition.

In order that people move themselves according to their vision of life they have to discover their own source of power within the spiritual dimension of their being. Psychological knowledge of themselves is not enough to live a life of vision, freedom and creativity. To live a complete life people need to know themselves, and they need to know how to know themselves. Psychology does not help us to know ourselves fully. Psychology provides us with theories to understand human behavior. As a science that tries to understand and predict behavior it works best when it is used for specific purposes, such as understanding the cognitive processes in learning or understanding the relationship between schizophrenia and genetic factors. As a science that is used to help people develop, it is used best in conjunction with philosophy and religious thought. However, today many people look to psychology for the answer to most if not all their concerns. People usually associate psychology with human growth, self-actualization and fulfillment. They look to psychology to find answers for problems relating to human communication, family development, love relationships, alcohol abuse and many other concerns. Although psychology can help with the psychological dimension of our concerns, the most important dimension of these concerns is often spiritual. By spiritual I mean the dimension of our being that reflects, intuits, chooses, creates and practices virtue.

Three last thoughts. First, throughout my formal education in counseling psychology I never experienced any serious demands made by the programs to examine the interaction of philosophy, psychology and religion within the person. The separate ways in which each of these disciplines is presented in most educational systems seems to say to the learner, "Pick one to guide your life." As a result people have difficulty understanding themselves as one united being with religious, philosophical and psychological concerns. Although this book does not academically address the question of the interaction among these three concerns within a person it does address in a practical way the interaction between a person's philosophy and psychology, while religion is touched on here and there.

Secondly, the style of this book is not academic, that is, not filled with references. Nor is the flavor journalistic, sensory and anecdotal. I suppose expository, pragmatic and reflective are the best words to describe the style.

Finally, this book presents a framework, namely the Human Tendencies Profile, as a background against which the helper can see the direction in which the helpee is moving. The three major tendencies are the irrational tendency of confusion, the rational tendency of order and the supra-rational tendency of vision. All the other tendencies flow from these three basic tendencies. The objective of this book is to show the reader how to help their counselees identify the tendencies in the background of their lives that are affecting their actions in the foreground of their lives. This book also shows the reader how to help their counselees strengthen their rational and supra-rational tendencies by demonstrating strategies and techniques for improving rational, empirical and intuitive thinking.

Choosing a Theory that Suits the Helpee

The first methodical step on the part of the helper in all theoretical approaches to counseling is observation. The helper observes the helpee and his world by using the techniques of attentive listening, reflecting the helpee's feelings and asking questions that stimulate self-exploration on the part of the helpee. In this first step, the helper gets in touch with the helpee's feelings, thoughts, and behaviors. The helper feels and sees how the helpee experiences himself and his world.

The next step is to guide the helpee to observe himself, that is, to look at himself subjectively, so that he can label his thoughts, feelings and behaviors as he is experiencing himself and his world. Writing out one's self-talk about a concern gives the helpee a chance to identify his emotions, behaviors, and thoughts, such as frustration, blaming and wishful thinking. The helpee can also get in touch with his values as well as his unreasonable assumptions and expectations, such as his value of excellence in work performance and his erroneous assumptions that all people value what he values with the same intensity.

At this point the helper needs to decide what theoretical approach will be most useful for the helpee. Once the helper knows the thoughts, emotions and behaviors of the helpee regarding a particular concern, the helper can identify the helpee's predominant irrational tendency. A tendency is a movement made from a combination of emotions, behaviors and thoughts. For example, if a helpee feels angry toward his boss, subtly sabotages his boss's projects and thinks himself superior in intellect to his boss, then the helpee probably experiences rebellion as his dominant irrational tendency. By asking the question, "Which tendencies on this chart do you prefer to experience while at work?," the helper will stimulate the helpee to get in touch, at least momentarily, with his rational and supra-rational tendencies. The helper and helpee will have set up their work.

Irrational	Rational	Supra-Rational
confusion	order	vision
dependence	control	freedom
rebellion	system	change
skepticism	certainty	creativity
(move down toward)	(move toward)	(move up toward)
self-destruction	self-profit	making our world

Helpee: I'm feeling rebellion. If I keep going this way, I'll destroy my self. I want to get some control of the situation and I want to feel free and creative at work.

Helper: (What is the best way to help him move from rebellion to freedom and creativity?)

The helper can focus on the emotion, behavior or thinking of the helpee. If an abundance of irrational thinking is inflaming the helpee's rebellion, then the helper might want to use a cognitive approach such as rational emotive therapy. If the helpee is not completely in touch with his anger and thinks of himself poorly, then a client-centered approach may be more useful. If the helpee thinks rationally and has a positive concept of himself, his rebellion may be more due to his lack of interpersonal skills with authority figures. Then, a behavioral approach may be more useful. What the helper is looking for at this point is the best psychological approach to bring about positive movement in the helpee's psychological dimension.

Before moving on with the psychological theory, the helper needs to explore with the helpee the helpee's philosophy of life. The helper does this by asking the helpee what he values most in his life. The point of this exercise is to help the helpee articulate his deepest feelings about life in the form of ideals. His articulated philosophy of life will be the compass that guides his psychological journey. He will have a clear *conceptual* vision of himself and his work. The next step is to move psychologically toward that vision.

A particular psychological mode, such as, client-centered therapy, rational emotive therapy or a succession of these counseling modes will be the vehicle for that journey. The goal of the helpee is to live his vision existentially, that is, moment by moment. The goal of the counselor is to cooperate with the helpee in discovering how to translate his vision into action.

Chapter II

THE ROOTS OF CONFUSION

Confusion means different things to us at different times. In adolescence we feel confused about ourselves. Our feelings of confusion raise questions like, "Who am I? What is right and what is wrong? What do I really believe in? Who can I trust?" Our questions push us to search for clarity. As we move on in life we occasionally feel confused about our relationships and work. We thought we were clear about our relationship with our parents. As they grow old and we grow old, we seem to be the parents, and they seem to be the children. We thought we were clear about our relationship to our children. As they mature they go through their stages of experimentation that put our trust in them to the test.

We thought we were clear about our relationship to our spouse. In the mid-thirties and early forties our spouse's sudden transformations throw us into confusion. The changes in our mid-thirties and forties appear abrupt, but the conditions of the changes were buried below the surface. We thought we were clear about our work. Now we feel stagnant. We look for a more exciting and challenging career. Luckily, we don't experience all these confusions at once. However, when we are confused about ourselves, then that confusion, like the fog rolling in from the sea, spreads to all the areas of our lives.

People seeking help are immediately aware of their confusion, but they are not in touch with the roots of that confusion. By crystalizing their thoughts in the forms of the following theories, they will understand how they drifted into confusion.

7

1. Ideal-self versus the real self

We all have a picture of ourselves as we would like to be. Our heroes in real life embody some of the characteristics of our ideal-self. We admire the courageous person, the intelligent person, the confident person, the creative person, the powerful person, the compassionate person, the serene person and the loving person. In the presence of our heroes we vacillate between admiration and a subtle envy that whispers, "Why can't you be like that." The more we focus on the *gap* between the way we perceive ourselves now and the way we would like to be, the more disappointed we become with ourselves. We begin to move toward confusion when we look for the models of our ideal self outside of ourselves. This type of thinking spreads to other areas of our lives. We begin to look for the ideal career out there, the ideal romance out there, the ideal marriage out there, the ideal family out there. We begin to compare our real self and our real relationships with the ideal models out there. Usually, we come out second best.

A feeling of impotence creeps into our real self. We begin to feel anxious, frustrated and confused. Our confusion begins when we let go of our intuition, self-reflection, ultimate choice and creativity. Intuition gives birth to an ideal concept. We represent in ideas what we deeply feel about ourselves in our intuition, such as the ideas of a loving person, a courageous person and a creative person. The challenge is to make ourselves into what *we* feel about ourselves through our powers of self-reflection, creativity and ultimate choice. Our confusion begins when we try to copy someone else's life. We cannot create ourselves by copying. Imitating and modeling are good behaviors for developing skills, but they are devastating behaviors in making our personality.

Another source of confusion is shaping our ideal self according to someone else's expectations of us. It is not uncommon that people have let their parents, their society and/or their religion construct an ideal self-concept for them. As they measure up to the demands placed on them they spend most of their lives living in internal confusion while appearing externally in control.

We can help people get out of their confusion by moving them toward an experience of their intuition. Then they will see that their intuition is an activity of the real self and their ideal self is the creative product of *their* real self. We can use the metaphor of the mountain climber to demonstrate the connection between the real self and the ideal self. The mountain climber tosses his line to a higher ledge where he envisions himself to be. Then, he moves. In life the real and intuitive self creates an ideal self. The real self projects the ideal self out in front of itself and then moves toward making the ideal through its powers of self-reflection and ultimate choice. The real self decides to move and plans its moves. The real and the ideal coincide at a point, and, then, the process starts over, just as the mountain climber begins again to look for a higher ledge.

Cues indicating that the root of confusion is the conflict between the real self and the ideal self:

"I just can't seem to make my parents happy."

"I can never measure up to my spouse's expectations of me."

"I've always been average. Everyone else seems to have something special."

"I wish someone could tell me the purpose of my life."

"I've been doing what I'm supposed to do, and it's not paying off."

"I dream about having a happy life. That's all it is...a dream."

The following types of thinking are behind these statements:
--comparative thinking = "Other people are better than I am."
--wishful thinking = "I dream about..."
--mechanical thinking = "I did what I was supposed to do."
--standards thinking = "I can't measure up to his expectations."
As the helpee gets in touch with his intuition he will begin to use other types of thinking, such as:
--metaphorical thinking (instead of comparative thinking) = "I am like a mountain climber."
--pragmatic thinking (instead of wishful thinking) = "What does the ideal of love mean for me in this situation?"

2. The unconscious dimension versus the conscious dimension of ourselves

The movement of human life is like the movement of a river. The river's beginning is modest. As it moves along, its banks stretch farther apart, and its bed falls deeper into the earth. Streams and brooks join this gentle and ponderous flow of water. Its destination is the vast ocean. The beginning of human life is humble. As we grow our life is fed by numerous experiences. Many of those experiences sink below our conscious life to move in a hidden way in the depths of our being. Both the movement of our conscious and unconscious dimensions are contained within cultural, social and religious bound-ries, just as the river is contained within its banks. But as the con-scious and unconscious dimensions of our life flow into the sea of Being, our life moves freely without boundaries.

The rational tendency to put everything in order and to control everything, so that we will feel secure and certain, can make us suspi-cious and fearful of the hidden, unknown, mysterious side of life. We prefer to dam up the flow of life and to swim on the surface of our shallow reservoir of conscious experiences.

When we believe that we have stopped the movement of Life, we feel that we are in control. In time we realize that we have only been deceiving ourselves. The force of the movement of Life exceeds our power to contain it. Eventually the dam will burst. We cannot still the movement of Life either in the conscious or unconscious dimension of our lives. We can get rid of our fear of the unknown, if we exercise our spiritual powers of intuition and ultimate choice. Instead of fearing the unknown we will be curious about it. We will feel free to trust the movement of Life carrying us to the boundless sea of Life.

Our confusion begins when we start to deny and repress the sur-facing contents of our unconscious. We are afraid to embrace our passions, our ideals, our anxieties, and our deepest questions. We are afraid of the power of the divine within us and the cunning of the evil within us. We deny them both, lest we take a chance on letting them battle each other. We fear that evil will be the victor. However, the more we deny and repress what lies below and above the surface of our conscious life, the more we feel torn apart. By stubbornly and rigidly controlling our conscious life to exclude the experiences of the unconscious and the supra-conscious, we end up in confusion.

The following are some of the contents of the unconscious that we might keep out of our conscious life:

> *The unconscious God:* The hidden, the mysterious, the
> terrifying and the powerful God is the unconscious God.
> We prefer our conscious God, the one that we know in
> our terms. We prefer the God of laws and rules, so that
> we always know where we stand in our relationship to
> Him. We prefer the God of love, the Heavenly Father,
> who is always there to soothe us. The unconscious God
> disturbs our religious security. The unconscious God is
> the free God, controlled by no law. The unconscious
> God is the infinite and unpredictable Being that cannot be
> known in our terms. The unconscious God invites us to

move with Him. We prefer to *rest* with Him. The unconscious God is everywhere and nowhere in particular. Our conscious God is right there where we have placed Him and where we can find Him. We are afraid of the unconscious God, because the unconscious God threatens our "faith" in our conscious God.

Our racial heritage: No human being is a pure color. We are all mixtures. We all have some white in us, some black in us, some yellow in us, and some red in us. We can identify with other races because we all participate in the same Life. Just as there is one light that is refracted into colors by a prism, so also there is one Humanity that is divided into races by geography. In our unguarded moments our feelings of association with other races emerge in our consciousness. However, they are short-lived. Fear forces us to remember *who we* are. Then, we take our "proper position."

Our hero: The hero is the personification of our ideals. He is the one that overcomes the danger and the fear of failure. He is the one that makes a believer out of a cynic. He is the one that proves that love, trust, loyalty and goodness are real and powerful. We keep the hero buried deep within our unconscious. If we allowed such an idea to influence our conscious life, for sure we would disrupt the smooth flow of our functional life. Our advice to ourselves is, "Don't be a hero. Don't rock the boat." Instead, we satisfy the movement in our unconscious by reading about fictional heroes or watching movies that glorify physical heroism. Our pragmatic view of life persuades us not to be a hero to ourselves.

Our passions: If we allow ourselves to be moved by the force of Life, we experience passion. We are seized, lifted up, thrown down, and projected ahead by the currents of Life, just as if we were riding the rapids of a wild river. In passion we experience the heights of joy and the pits of emptiness. At one moment we are riding high. In the next moment we feel ourselves falling into nothingness. We feel powerless. Our only hope is to trust the Life that is moving us along. In passion we discover sin, and we discover love. We cannot know love without sin, and we cannot know sin without love. In passion we see that sin is the absence of trust in Life. Sin means to be more concerned about ourselves, that is, about our purity, about our pleasure, or about our reputation than about Life. Love means to give oneself to Life, to trust in the ultimate goodness of Life, and to allow one's consciousness to be inspired by the movements of Life in one's unconsciousness.

3. Moving versus rest

Our expectation for rest is probably the most persistent source of our confusion. Life can become a series of resting places. As we look back on each place, we thought that we were satisfied, fulfilled, and altogether. We had the best job and the best marriage. Then, the unexpected happens and spoils it for us. The economy turns sour, or we develop new needs that must be satisfied. Our job no longer exists or has become boring. Our spouse gets careless and ceases to measure up to our expectations. If our goal is to have it all and then to rest in our possessions, we will end up feeling confused, as soon as we discover that we don't have it all.

Living means to make beauty rather than to have things. The making of beauty is an ongoing process. The artist does not create in order to make a final work in which he can rest. On the contrary, each work expands his horizon. He is inspired to move on. So also, humans are inspired to move on as they create beauty in their world. If we look for satisfaction, we will be discouraged and confused. If we look to make beauty, we will be encouraged and inspired.

4. Types of thinking as a source of confusion

The ways in which we think can become a source of confusion for us, if we don't reflect on our thinking. The three basic types of thinking are: empirical, rational and intuitive.

> *Empirical*: We think empirically when our sensations are the primary judges of what is true and false and what is good and bad. For example, true love for the empirical thinker, means pleasant sensations that come from having our psychological needs satisfied with physical things. We know that we are loved when our need for security is satisfied by the adulation provided by our lover, and when our need for belonging and affection are satisfied with sex provided by our lover.

Rational: We think rationally when logical consistency is the primary judge of what is true and false and what is good and bad. For example, true love means that the moral and psychological contract in which two people agree to be there for each other, to respect each other and to be loyal to each other will guide their attitudes toward each other.

Intuitive: We think intuitively when we use symbolic representations to grasp intellectually what we deeply feel. For example, we try to express in a symbol, such as a broken heart, our deepest feelings concerning the harmony and the unity of love as well as the suffering and the paradoxes of love. If we cannot create a symbol within our own creative imagination, we will search for one created by someone else in music, poetry or literature.

Many people skillfully use all three ways of thinking in making a beautiful life without labeling the type of thinking that they are using. Thinking in these three ways without thinking about our thinking is similar to playing the piano by ear. The piano player intuitively knows the difference between noise and music. When he is making noise, then he knows that it's time to think about what he is doing. He now theorizes about music before playing it. In living life we intuitively know the difference between ugliness and beauty. When we are experiencing ugliness, then we know it's time to think about our thinking.

We feel confused because we do not intend to make the ugliness that we experience. If we think about the type of thinking that we are doing when we feel confused, we will discover that the distortions that we are experiencing about ourselves and our relationships are usually the result of our imbalance in our three types of thinking. For example, suppose that we believe that fulfillment is measured by pleasant sensations. If a surgeon were to use that same type of thinking exclusively in performing a heart bypass, he would be disgusted by the goriness of it all. However, the surgeon also has an intuitive and rational viewpoint telling him that the entire surgical event is a work of art. Although this example is rather simplistic, it does show how our thinking contributes to the content of our experiences. In relating to ourselves and to other people the interplay of these three types of thinking is rapid and subtle. However, with regular reflection we can get in touch with our usual way of thinking. The empirical way of thinking, that is, relying on sensation to tell us what is true or false, is generally used more than the other two types. For example, if we are not consistently receiving pleasant sensations in a relationship, then we will probably feel confused about the other person's "feelings" toward us, such as—"Do my children really love me'—"Do my parents really love me?"—"Does my spouse really love me?"—We even begin to wonder about our own intentions, because at times we feel repelled by the selfishness, laziness and inattentiveness of the person that we love. At certain times we do not like them, because we do not have pleasant sensations of them. When we have an imbalance in our thinking, we experience distortion. Our types of thinking are like three spokes on a wheel. If they are unequal, we get a distorted wheel.

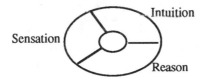

If the spokes are equal, we get a balanced wheel.

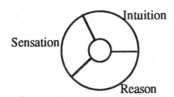

In helping people we discover that balancing our thinking is not as simple as mechanically adjusting the spokes of a wheel. The hub of the wheel represents the spiritual dimension of our being. There, we are free to choose how we will think. Some people choose to live an imbalanced life. They moan and groan about the bumpy road of life, while deep within themselves they know that it is not the road, it is their "wheel of life" that is distorted.

Chapter III

A Practical Introduction To The Human Tendencies Profile

Everybody likes to help each other. We feel good when we have done something for someone. Everybody believes in ideals like love, justice and honest communication. And almost everyone believes that a full and joyful life requires giving oneself to another person. However, most of us experience a gap between the ideals that we believe in and our daily experiences. Some people put out an enormous amount of effort to help people, yet they *don't* feel good about themselves or the people they are trying to help. Other people *only believe* in the ideal of helping others, but put out little effort to respond to someone else's need intelligently. Then, there are those people that reasonably actualize their ideals of love and justice in helping somebody. Their positive feelings toward themselves and toward the people that they help grow stronger as they close the gap between the ideal and the real. What makes the difference between the successful helper and the unsuccessful helper? More specifically, what is the difference between:

-- a helping parent and a non-helping parent?
-- a helping spouse and a non-helping spouse?
-- a helping teacher and a non-helping teacher?
-- a helping friend and a non-helping friend?
-- a helping boss and a non-helping boss?
-- a helping counselor and a non-helping counselor?

Before we can answer our question we have to settle on the basic meaning of helping. I will propose the following meaning: *to help another person means to cooperate with that person in realizing his vi-*

15

sion of himself and of life. There are many levels of helping, but the most fundamental meaning is to cooperate with the person trying to actualize his vision.

The following are simple but major ideas involved in the process of helping a person:

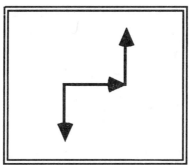

1. *Living means to move in some direction* - We are moving down, moving along or moving up.

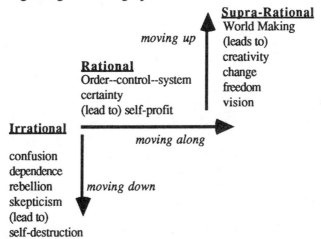

2. *We have tendencies that move us down, along or move us up.*[*]

---

[*]From Jason, K. and McMahon, J., *The Power to Change Your Life* (New York: Doubleday, 1982).

Generally speaking, helping means to cooperate with someone in actualizing his vision. Specifically, helping has different meanings, since the helpee can be moving down toward self-destruction, moving along toward self-profit or moving up toward world-making. For example, a husband and wife may be helping each other to actualize their shared vision of a happy family. If both are in touch with their supra-rational tendencies of vision, freedom, change and creativity then helping means dialoguing with each other to discover practical ways of realizing their ideals of unity and love that characterize a happy family.

If, in another case, one spouse experiences a dominating irrational tendency, such as confusion about his or her identity and the other spouse is in touch with his or her own vision about his or her own identity, then helping means that the spouse in touch with his or her vision does what is necessary to cooperate with the spouse experiencing confusion, so that the confused person will get in touch with his or her rational tendency of order and ultimately vision.

The first step in the helping process is to become aware of the tendencies that the helpee is experiencing in a particular aspect of his life. For example, if the helpee is experiencing a great deal of confusion that can spread to other areas of his life. He will start to lose confidence in himself. In a short time he will become overly dependent on other people. To stop the downward slide he has to admit his confusion. His next step is to get in touch with his vision of himself. Afterwards, he will be able to construct some realistic goals for his career or relationships.

The following three concentric circles illustrate the components of the helping experience:

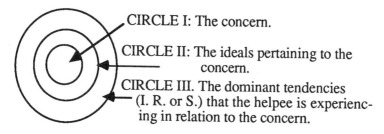

CIRCLE I: The concern.

CIRCLE II: The ideals pertaining to the concern.

CIRCLE III. The dominant tendencies (I. R. or S.) that the helpee is experiencing in relation to the concern.

Suppose the helpee is concerned about his relationship with one of his teenage children. Let's describe the content of each circle and the interactions among the circles.

Circle I - The Concern: The helpee finds it is difficult to talk with his teenage son about his school work, his social life and almost anything touching on a personal conversation. The helpee feels that he and his son are drifting apart. He feels that he ought to do something to warm up the cool atmosphere between himself and his son.

Circle II - The Ideals: The helpee feels that he ought to do something about his relationship with his son, because his intuition that is in touch with his ideals in Circle II is telling him that the relationship is not right. *Ideals are like stars in the night that tell us where we are and where we are headed on the sea of life. Ideals are not pictures of what we are supposed to be.* The helpee's intuitive attachment to his ideals of paternal love and care tell him that he is off course. He seems to be moving away from his son.

Circle III - The Dominant Tendencies: Circle III is the place where the foundation of the helping process is built. First, the helper and the helpee have to get in touch with their own emotions, thoughts and behaviors. If the father is seeking help from a friend, then the friend ought to reflect the emotions, behaviors and thoughts of the father to the father. For example, after a lengthy discussion the friend might summarize the father's thoughts, feelings and behaviors by saying, "You seem to feel frustrated because you are trying to draw out your son by initiating conversations about his life, but he clams up and tries to avoid you at times. Sometimes you feel angry with him. I guess you are depending on him to open up, so that you will feel better about the relationship."

In diagram form we have the following:

CIRCLE I. The concern: The Father-son relationship is not good.

CIRCLE II. Father is in touch with the ideal of parental love.

CIRCLE III. The dominant tendency of the father is irrational dependency. To feel like a good caring father, he depends on the positive responses of his son.

In Circle III the helpee experiences all three types of tendencies, irrational, rational and supra-rational. However, when we are experiencing a concern in Circle I, we simultaneously feel a dominant tendency in Circle III. In the example, the father is experiencing a dominant irrational tendency of dependence in relation to his son. However, in his career he may be experiencing dominant rational tendencies with his colleagues.

At this point we have to say a word about the friend that is functioning as a helper to the father. The helper has to stay in touch with his supra-rational tendencies and rational tendencies in the process of helping. Remember, helping means to cooperate with a person in actualizing *his* vision of life. In our example the friend sees that the father is not in touch with his supra-rational tendency of vision. The father's ideals in Circle II, which are supposed to function like stars fixing his position on the sea of life are useless, because in Circle III he is moving around irrationally with his eyes cast down on the deck of the ship. He has to see his ideals, not simply know that they are there. And he has to choose a direction guided by his ideals. Ideals are not magnets pulling our ship into port. The goal of the helper, therefore, in Circle III is to cooperate with the helpee in assessing the tendencies that he is experiencing. To achieve his goal the helper must concentrate on his own supra-rational and rational tendencies. Good intentioned people trying to help others fall into the trap of telling the helpee what to do. The helpee can easily become dependent on the advice of the person trying to help. If the helpee is moving downward, that is, experiencing dominating irrational tendencies, then the goal of the helper is to cooperate with the helpee so that the helpee will put into gear his own rational and supra-rational tendencies in resolving his concern in Circle I. Once the helpee, the father in our example, is in touch with his vision and freedom in Circle III, he will see that what he was doing in Circle I was inconsistent with the ideals of love and parental care in Circle II. While experiencing the irrational tendency of dependence, he was probably crowding his son and behaving manipulatively to actualize his ideal of parental love. If he is in touch with his vision and freedom, he will change his behaviors and thoughts toward his son. He will realize that loving and caring for his son means to cooperate with his son, so that his son will get in touch with his own rational and supra-rational tendencies. Instead of pressuring his son to open up, the father might have to learn how to attend patiently to his son.

Initial response of father to son - impatience and crowding.

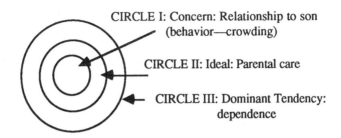

CIRCLE I: Concern: Relationship to son
(behavior—crowding)

CIRCLE II: Ideal: Parental care

CIRCLE III: Dominant Tendency:
dependence

Changed response of the father to son - patiently attending.

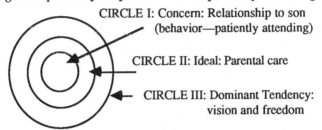

CIRCLE I: Concern: Relationship to son
(behavior—patiently attending)

CIRCLE II: Ideal: Parental care

CIRCLE III: Dominant Tendency:
vision and freedom

The father first changed his tendency in Circle III from dependence
to vision.

Human Tendencies Profile

Irrational	Rational	Supra-Rational
confusion	order	vision
dependence	control	freedom
rebellion	system	change
skepticism	certainty	creativity
(move down toward)	(move toward)	(move up toward)
self-destruction	self-profit	making our world

Psychology and Beyond Psychology

His hand gently clasping her hand moved rhythmically with hers. The
two hands moved as one. The knife as if it were a living extension of
their hands moved steadily and easily through the cake. First, one cut
from the center to the circumference. Then, another cut from the
center to the circumference made with the same gracefully unified
hands. Without he or she saying a word to each other, their hands

moved in harmony. Their words were in their touch. Together they offered the first slice of thier fortieth wedding anniversary cake to their first great-grandchild.

The above vignette depicts enduring love, flourishing love, and deep love, that curious and beautiful phenomenon at any age. We all want to know the secret of enduring and growing love. Mature people experiencing mature love testify to the truth that enduring love is nurtured by diligence, attention, good will and thoughtfulness. If by "secret" we mean an easy way, then there is no secret for experiencing true love. People that believe in an easy way to love live with illusions of love. If by secret we mean insights that help humans love genuinely, then we can learn from other people's experiences as well as our own.

This book addresses the question, "How do we help people that want to make their ideals real?" The ideal of love, unlike the illusion of love, can guide us to the psychological experience of love. However, if we want to experience love psychologically, we must stay in touch with the ideal of love through our spiritual powers of intuition, self-reflection, creativity and ultimate choice. For example, if on the psychological level we want to experience the emotions of joy and tranquility associated with true love, then on the spiritual level we need to stay in touch with our intuition of love telling us that love is generous, love is kind, love, is understanding love is courageous and love is giving. We also need to reaffirm daily our ultimate choice to love, that is, to decide to do what in the end finally counts, to love. In answering our question, "How can we help people to realize their ideals?"—we will examine the *content* of our irrational, rational and supra-rational tendencies and the *interactions* among these tendencies. We will also see how our psychological and spiritual processes affect each other as they strengthen or weaken certain tendencies.

Let's illustrate these ideas by going to our example of the father who is concerned about his relationship to his son. The following diagram shows the content and interactions among the tendencies and the effects that the psychological and spiritual processes have on the development of these tendencies.

Stage 1
Dominant tendency of father in relation to son.
Dependence
  Content of irrational tendency of dependency: seeks son's attention in order to feel good as a concerned father; without son's attention, he feels that he is failing as a father.

Interaction between irrational and rational tendencies: uses rational tendencies of order and control to get his son to respond to him. Puts parental pressure on son because his feelings about himself depend on son's response.

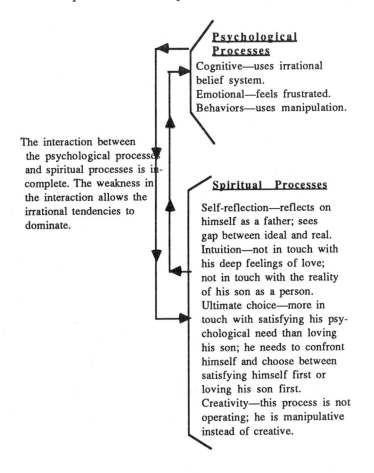

Psychological Processes

Cognitive—uses irrational belief system.
Emotional—feels frustrated.
Behaviors—uses manipulation.

The interaction between the psychological processes and spiritual processes is incomplete. The weakness in the interaction allows the irrational tendencies to dominate.

Spiritual Processes

Self-reflection—reflects on himself as a father; sees gap between ideal and real.
Intuition—not in touch with his deep feelings of love; not in touch with the reality of his son as a person.
Ultimate choice—more in touch with satisfying his psychological need than loving his son; he needs to confront himself and choose between satisfying himself first or loving his son first.
Creativity—this process is not operating; he is manipulative instead of creative.

Stage II: *After the change*
Dominant tendencies in relation to son: Vision Freedom
   Content: sees son as a person in himself; sees himself as someone that wants to be with his son for his own sake; feels free to let his son be himself; searches for new ways to reach his son.

Interaction: The order, that is, the pattern of thoughts and behaviors in his relationship with his son is guided by his attentiveness to his son; the son also exercises some control in the relationship.

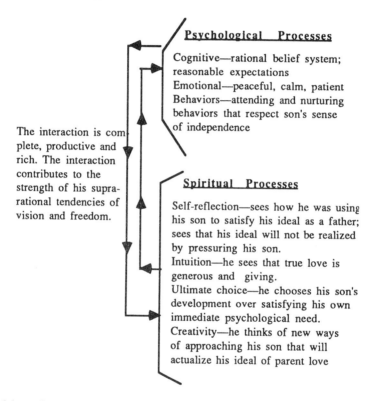

Psychological Processes

Cognitive—rational belief system; reasonable expectations
Emotional—peaceful, calm, patient
Behaviors—attending and nurturing behaviors that respect son's sense of independence

The interaction is complete, productive and rich. The interaction contributes to the strength of his supra-rational tendencies of vision and freedom.

Spiritual Processes

Self-reflection—sees how he was using his son to satisfy his ideal as a father; sees that his ideal will not be realized by pressuring his son.
Intuition—he sees that true love is generous and giving.
Ultimate choice—he chooses his son's development over satisfying his own immediate psychological need.
Creativity—he thinks of new ways of approaching his son that will actualize his ideal of parent love

Although we use our psychological knowledge, much of which we acquire through common sense, to cooperate with each other, we also use our rational and intuitive knowledge in helping people. Our psychological knowledge is like the functional knowledge that we have of the ship on the high seas. Our rational and intuitive knowledge is like the knowledge that we have of the stars and the sea. Just as the seaman needs both kinds of knowledge to navigate his way on the boundless oceans, so also we need to know how we function psychologically, and we need to know how to find our direction in life. Psychological knowledge alone is not enough to live a complete life. Just as a ship may be functioning well as it goes around in circles, so also we may function well psychologically without any clear sense of direction. At some point we might feel bored and frustrated, because we are moving in circles. Boredom is a psychological response for not using our rational and intuitive knowledge to set a course for our lives. We feel most alive when we are moving toward our envisioned destination. If we accept the idea that human life at its highest level is self-generated positive movement, then the metaphor of the seaman navigating his ship through the high ocean waves on his way to his destination will make sense. There are some obvious shortcomings with this metaphor. However, the point of the metaphor is to show that human life at its best is experienced as positive movement. And we require psychological and spiritual knowledge of ourselves to move ourselves positively.

The Purpose of this Book

The purpose of this book is to show how to use the principles, methods and skills of the helping process in cooperating with people experiencing dominant irrational tendencies. Our question is, "How do we help people move from confusion, dependence, rebellion and skepticism about themselves and others to vision, freedom, change and creativity in order to make a better world for themselves and others?" If we can give a good theoretical answer, and if we can apply our theory effectively, then we will be successful helpers.

Movement in life is impeded by the malfunctioning of physical, psychological and spiritual processes. A problem in one dimension could have an effect in another dimension. For example, a brain tumor may affect the psychological processes of cognition and emotion. We may have difficulty in remembering, and we may feel depressed. In a reverse order we may experience depression, because psychologically we have difficulties imaging ourselves positively. Then we will experience the physical effects of our depression. We will feel fatigued. We will eat poorly. We will sleep excessively. Perhaps we can trace our poor self-image to the lack of affection and acceptance on the part of our parents. With the assistance of a professional psychologist we can learn to understand our depression and to overcome it by developing a positive self-image. Finally, we have difficulties that are rooted in the malfunctioning of our spiritual processes. By spiritual processes I mean the activities of intuition, reflection, ultimate choice and creativity. If these activities are not operating at full throttle, we will experience negative psychological and physical consequences.

The point of this book is to show people how to cooperate with each other to activate and strengthen their spiritual processes, so that they will know how to maintain strong supra-rational tendencies. As we said before, what we do in one dimension of our lives affects the other two dimensions. If we want to help people develop strong supra-rational tendencies, we need to know how they are functioning psychologically and spiritually. For example, if a person is experiencing a strong irrational tendency of skepticism that is destroying him we need to discover what psychological processes are malfunctioning and what factors, such as past experiences with parents, friends and others, contributed to the development of his lack of trust in himself and others. Once the psychological obstacles are cut down to manageable sizes, our next step is to cooperate with the person to stimulate his spiritual powers of intuition, self-reflection, ultimate choice and creativity.

I am using the word spiritual to distinguish a dimension of our being which is different from the psychological dimension. Spiritual does not mean religious, although religious could be incorporated into a person's spiritual dimension. In this century we are in the habit of putting all human activities in two categories: physical and psychological. Religion for many people falls outside these categories. So some religious people are suspicious of psychology, and some psychologists are suspicious of religion. But there is another dimension to us, the spiritual dimension. We can be spiritually religious, which is true religion, and psychologically religious, which is usually false religion. By psychologically religious I mean that our religious behaviors, such as going to church are motivated by fear, anxiety or selfish interests. By doing religious rituals we get a psychological payoff. We feel good because we did what we were supposed to do. I am parenthetically bringing up the topic of religion here, because some people confuse the idea of spiritual with the idea of religious. Let's keep in mind that helping in the context of this book means to cooperate with people in *discovering, strengthening* and *using* their supra-rational tendencies to make a better world for themselves and others.

Different books have different effects on people. Some books soothe and comfort wounded souls. Some books entertain. They give the weary traveler a rest. Some books enlighten and challenge us. They confront us with different perspectives or with a slightly different angle on life. The purpose of this book is to enlighten and challenge people interested in helping others to function well both psychologically and spiritually.

Those in the helping professions, such as counselors, ministers, social workers, and teachers know that helping others requires patience, professional knowledge and self-knowledge. So, this book is written in non-technical language for people interested in acquiring patience, some professional knowledge and some self-knowledge so that they can be more helpful to others on an interpersonal level. The different perspective of this book is that it looks at helping people from the viewpoint of the Human Tendencies Profile. People starting out in the helping professions that have adopted an eclectic approach to helping others can use the Human Tendencies Profile as a superstructure guiding their choice of theory. The following diagram illustrates the challenge facing the helper in the context of our human tendencies.

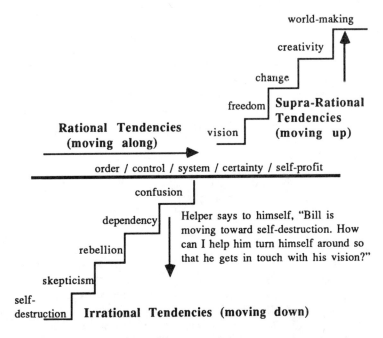

The Origin of the Human Tendencies Profile

You might be wondering about the origin of the Human Tendencies Profile. Where did it come from? The ideas of tendency, irrational, rational and supra-rational are used in many psychological theories and philosophies. The particular pattern of selected tendencies in the Human Tendencies Profile is the result of my search for a superstructure that would help me understand how humans move in life. I used the chart with people that I counseled or taught to see if it made sense to them. After people talked about their concerns and about their thoughts, emotions and behaviors relating to their concerns, I would ask them if any of the tendencies on the Human Tendencies Profile described what they were experiencing. Almost all of the hundreds of people using the chart could label their global experiences relating to a particular concern by pointing to a tendency. They would say something like, "There I am," (pointing to dependence). "I want to be over there," (pointing to freedom). Then, the challenge of working together to move from dependence to freedom presented itself. The next question for me was, "What counseling theory or theories would be most effective with this person to help him reach his goal of experiencing freedom in relation to his particular concern at this time." So, the Human Tendencies Profile has been developed from my experience in teaching psychology and philosophy and from the responses of counselees, students and colleagues using the profile.

Chapter IV

The Just and Loving Relationship

The goal of helping people is to cooperate with them in discovering how to love themselves and in discovering how to create loving relationships with the people in their world. People suffer because they do not know how to love themselves or others. To help means to engage in a dialogue with people seeking enlightenment so that they will discover how to make love a reality in themselves and in their relationships. As helpers we have to ask ourselves the question, "What is a true loving relationship?" Before looking into theories, techniques and strategies of helping, let's answer that question. If we want to help someone we need to have clear, true and useful concepts about love.

A true loving relationship is a just relationship. Frequently both parties in a relationship suffer injustices at the hands of each other in the name of love. We breach many fine lines. At first we tolerate the shortcomings of a friend, then we wink at his injustices lest we offend him and lose a friend. At first we behave righteously in correcting the misbehavior of our children, then we allow our anger full rein when they annoy us. At first we care for our children, so that they will develop into their own persons; then we pamper them, so that we do not lose their approval. At first we listen attentively to our colleague's concerns to help him resolve his difficulties, then we condone his poor judgements about people. At first we respect the freedom of our spouse to make his/her career decisions, then we become benignly indifferent. Each time that we cross the line dividing waning virtue from incipient vice we rationalize our move in the name of love: "I close my eyes to his drinking. After all, love is blind"; "I get angry at

29

you because I love you so much"; and "A friend is a friend no matter what he does."

Justice separates true love from false love. To grasp the meaning of justice imagine a community of people that uses good judgement in expressing its concern for each other. Imagine that the behaviors of the people in this community are congruent with their intentions to love each other. There would be no strife, anger, hostility, indifference or permissiveness. There would be differences, misunderstandings and frustrations. But, the characteristics of this community would be movement toward compassion, harmony, symmetry, consistency, balance, proportion and strength. It would be a just community, and a just community is a beautiful community.

When we use the word justice, we are talking about the verbal and behavioral expressions of our intention to love. The relationship between love and justice is similar to the relationship between the vision of the artist and his work. The vision of the artist far exceeds a particular work. But, his work expressing harmony, symmetry, proportion and strength is a true and just expression of his vision. Although we can appreciate the beauty of his work, only the artist knows how genuine it is, that is, how close it comes to expressing his vision. Likewise, in making our lives, only we know how genuine, true and just our expressions of love are. Love is our intention to actualize our intuitive vision of unity. Justice is our genuine expression of that intention. Justice means harmony between our intentions and actions. Justice means to act consistently according to our vision of love. Justice means to act courageously for the sake of truth and goodness. Justice means to act prudently, so that we develop a sense of balance and proportion. A true, loving relationship, that is, a relationship shaped by the intention of unity is a just relationship. If we keep our minds on the meaning of justice as we described it above, it will keep us honest in our actions towards others.

Reward and punishment is another meaning for justice. This meaning of justice is based on the idea of exchange. In other words we get back what we dish out. If we do good, we are rewarded; if we do evil, we are punished. This idea of justice is not based on a vision of unconditional love. The justice of reward and punishment is a minimal kind of justice that is not an expression of our vision of love. The justice of reward and punishment has little room for reconciliation, forgiveness and generosity. When we speak of a truly just relationship, we do not mean a relationship based on exchange. A just relationship means a relationship that is made according to the vision of unconditional love.

Distorted Love Versus Authentic Love

Love is the relentless force moving us to care for one another. Instinctively we rush to help someone in trouble. Deep within us we feel the urge to do something worthwhile for another person. Whenever we respond unselfishly to our conscience pointing the way to help someone, we feel spiritually good. Love is the *unconscious* attraction toward others that we mysteriously feel, *and* love is the *conscious* intention to unite ourselves spiritually, physically and psychologically with others.

The power of the unconscious attraction to unite with another person churns endlessly in the depths of our being. The force of this attraction is enormous and that is why we constantly yearn to *be* loved, to *be* accepted, and to feel secure. However, if love for us always means to *be* loved, and if we do not *actively* and *consciously* direct our deep seated feelings to unite with others, we will experience distortions in our relationships.

The Human Tendencies Profile can help us judge whether our helping relationships are just and empowering or whether they are distorted and manipulative. The chart contains three types of human tendencies, that is, movements within us toward self-destruction, self-profit and world-making.

Human Tendencies Profile

Irrational	Rational	Supra-Rational
confusion	order	vision
dependence	control	freedom
rebellion	system	change
skepticism	certainty	creativity
(move down toward)	(move toward)	(move up toward)
self-destruction	self-profit	making our world

We move progressively through the tendencies in each group. For example, in the column of irrational tendencies, we first experience the irrational tendency of confusion and then we experience dependence and so on down the column. When we are confused about ourselves or an important issue, we experience the next irrational tendency of dependence. Since we don't know the answer to our problem, we are ready to depend on someone to give us the answer. If that answer doesn't work for us, then we are ready for the next irrational tendency of rebellion. When we get tired of rebelling we are ready for skepticism and cynicism. Finally, we are ready to accept the belief that life is meaningless.

In the column of rational tendencies order is the first tendency because reason looks for order first. We look for some principle to help us put our thoughts in order. Then we experience some control in our lives. We want all the areas of our lives to relate to each other harmoniously. Next, we begin to systematize our lives. If all goes well we experience a high degree of certainty and self-profit, at least regarding those things that we can control.

Our supra-rational tendencies feed on the fruits of our intuition. Our intuition, that is, our deepest feelings and flashes of insight about life, pushes us to symbolize those internal experiences more clearly. Consequently, vision is our first supra-rational tendency. The more we see, the more freedom we experience. We feel more powerful and mobile, because we see more possibilities for ourselves and others. Then, we are ready to make changes and to make them creatively. The end product is a new world that we have made.

The unconscious force of love distorts our helping relationships when our irrational tendencies of confusion, dependence, rebellion and skepticism dominate us. The most common distortion occurs when the helper depends on the helpee to be dependent on the helper. The common denominator, either conscious or unconscious, between the helper and the helpee is mutual dependency, even though on the surface of the relationship the helper appears to be rational and at times supra-rational. Let's see how our irrational tendencies distort our love.

1. The Family

The love between parents and children requires special care because children can easily become confused and dependent and because parents have natural authority and control over their children. However, children also have strong intuitive tendencies that need parental attention. What we have to say in this section applies with some reservations to children approximately between the ages of seven and eighteen.

Parents tend to be concerned about order and control in their relationships with their children. Too often the order and control are based on their own irrational tendencies and the irrational tendencies of their children. For example, parents will withhold their affection and attention in order to make their children obey them. This tactic confuses their children who deeply want to be united with their parents. The children allow themselves to become dependent on their parents' authority in order to get their parents' approval. The common denominator between parents and the children in the foregoing scenario is their irrational tendencies. The parents are confused about the meaning of parental authority, and the children are confused about their parents' feelings toward them. So the parents depend on their children's dependency for approval and acceptance in order to get order and control in the household. On the surface the unity between the children and the parents looks like love, but the relationship is distorted.

True order and control in a parent-child relationship comes from our rational and supra-rational tendencies. Our children at times are unruly and confused. The quick, easy and unreflecting response is to punish or to withdraw our affection. We rationalize our action by telling ourselves that what we are doing is for their own good and is out of love for them. "After all," we protest, "we are only helping them to grow up in the real world." It's more difficult to respond to our undisciplined children from our own rational and supra-rational tendencies. But true love means to cooperate with others in order to help them rationally actualize their supra-rational tendencies. Kids want to express their freedom, to do something new, and to see something different. The burden is on us to think of creative ways of responding to them so that they learn how to order and control their own lives according to their personal vision of life. The following diagram illustrates the interactions of tendencies that distort love and that actualize love:

1 Child	Parent—Distorted Love
Irrational tendency of rebellion. "Don't tell me what to do."	Rational tendency of order and control. "I'm telling you to do this for your own good. And if you don't do it you are no longer my son."

Common Denominator

(either conscious or unconscious)

Child —irrational tendency of rebellion and confusion.

Parent —irrational tendency of depending on child's tendency to be dependent on parent for acceptance.

In this interaction the parent's rational response on the surface is prompted by the dominant and underlying irrational tendency of dependency. The parent is trying to influence the child to change his behavior by depending on the power of parental authority or by depending on the child's dependency for approval. If the child changes, he receives the affection of his parents. They feel united, but the union rests on the shaky foundation of mutual irrational dependency. This kind of relationship is the seed for future guilt and anger that parents and grown children will feel towards each other.

2 Child	**Parent—Just Love**
Irrational tendency of rebellion. "Don't tell me what to do."	Rational tendency of order and control. "You have an idea about how to make your own decisions."

Common Denominator
(usually, the rational and supra-rational tendencies
in the denominator are conscious to both people.)

Child —rational tendency of order: "What idea do I have
about making my own decisions?"

Parent —rational tendency of control: "The only control
I have over him is to help him to think so that
he controls himself."

In this interaction the parent's rational response motivated by his underlying rational tendency helps the child to get in touch with his underlying rational tendencies. Authentic love will develop from this kind of interaction. Both the child and the parent will move to the next interaction of their supra-rational tendencies.

3 Child	Parent—Just Love
Rational tendency of order and certainty: "I wonder what makes a good decision?"	Supra-rational tendency of vision: "I guess you see what is imporant to you."

Common Denominator

Child —Supra-rational tendency of vision and freedom: "What is really important to me? It's up to me to make a choice."

Parent —Supra-rational tendency of vision and freedom: "I can share my insights with him, but he is free to make his choices."

In this interaction both the parent and the child according to their own abilities at their own stages of development are using their supra-rational tendencies of vision and freedom to put order in their relationship. Their relationship is resting firmly on the strong foundation of their vision and freedom instead of wavering precariously on the shifting sands of their irrational dependencies.

2. Romantic Relationships

Probably, love gets distorted more in romantic relationships than in any other kind of relationship. The emotional difficulties that we experience in a romantic relationship can tell us something about the quality and the reality of our sexual relationship with a person of the opposite sex. When real conflicts disturb the euphoric feelings of a romance, we are forced to face the true meaning of love.

True romance, that is, a truly affectionate and sexual relationship, cannot exist without true love. A love relationship is deeper, broader, and more consistent than a romantic relationship. True love is the fertile soil nurturing the flower of romantic love. But the garden of love has many other flowers, such as commitment, trust, patience, understanding and generosity to name but a few. As we said before, true love is the conscious intention to unite ourselves freely to another spiritually, psychologically and physically. Romance is a partial but a particular and passionate expression of union between a man and woman. Let's use the Human Tendencies Profile to show the difference between distorted love and real love in romance.

Human Tendencies Profile

Irrational	Rational	Supra-Rational
confusion	order	vision
dependence	control	freedom
rebellion	system	change
skepticism	certainty	creativity
(move down toward)	(move toward)	(move up toward)
self-destruction	self-profit	making our world

Romantic love is distorted love when the common denominator in a man-woman relationship is an irrational tendency. Usually, the distortion occurs because one or both persons are confused about their own identity, their values, their goals and their self-esteem. If both are confused about themselves then the physical attraction they feel toward each other makes them feel good psychologically. They depend on the physical attraction for the new order and control in their lives. They believe that they are "in love" because they are experiencing to some degree their intention to unite themselves to each other. If over time the force of the physical attraction weakens, one or both persons begin to rebel. They start their long journey to mutual self-destruction by using cutting remarks and distrust.

If one of the persons in the relationship is motivated by a strong irrational tendency and the other is more in touch with rational and supra-rational tendencies then the dynamics are different from the situation where both are motivated by irrational tendencies. On the surface both the man and the woman appear to be responding to each other rationally and supra-rationally at the outset of the romance. They seem to be waltzing joyfully and freely through life with a clear vision of their destination. As the waltz continues, one partner feels that he or she is dragging the other through the dance. One partner no longer seems to be listening to the music. The one that has stopped dancing wants to be carried through life. The person in touch with the rational and supra-rational tendencies realizes that the other person is irrationally dependent. A critical point in the relationship is reached when the rational person is aware of the other's irrational tendency. The music stops. Either the irrational person will get in touch with his rational and supra-rational tendencies, or the rational person will drift toward becoming irrational in order to accommodate himself to his partner, *or* one party will walk out of this relationship if there is no movement toward each other.

Romantic love is just, true and alive when it is nourished by true love. However, true love is made by a man and a woman responding to each other out of their supra-rational and rational tendencies. Both have a clear vision of themselves, and they feel free to express themselves spiritually, physically and psychologically. They are also ready to face conflicts and to solve them creatively and cooperatively. They do not irrationally depend on each other, instead they freely move with each other and continually encourage each other.

Helping: The Activity of Creating Just Relationships

Helping is an act of love. True helping is based on true love. And the source of true love is our supra-rational and rational tendencies. In helping people we must operate from our strength in order to lead people to their own source of strength. Just as love can become distorted in family and romantic relationships, it can also become distorted in helping relationships. Irrational tendencies dominate certain areas in the lives of the people that we help. We have to be careful that our own irrational tendencies do not unite with theirs.

Chapter V

Principles of Helping

To help means to give and to cooperate. First, let's talk about giving. Giving is the most joyful experience in life. Deep down we all desire to help each other, that is, to give our time and talents to advance the well-being of each other. Intuitively we know that the eternal law of life is to give. Giving is *the* human action that makes love a reality. When two people give themselves to each other, love is created. Although we know that giving is *the* most human action that makes living worthwhile, doing it does not come automatically or easily.

How many times have we tried to help someone only to be criticized by that same person for making matters worse? How many times have we tried to extend ourselves to someone only to be accused by that same person for not caring? How many times have we answered someone's call for help only to be told in word or in action by that same person, "You can't help"? Helping each other successfully is not an easy skill to master. Part of the difficulty is tied up with the images that we have about helping someone. If we think of simple examples, we would probably come up with a list resembling the following:

I helped a blind man across the street.

I helped the little old lady with her heavy package.

I helped up the man that slipped on the ice.

I gave him a hand to push his car out of the snow.

I helped my son with his homework.

39

In most of the examples like the above we are doing something *for* or *to* someone. Even in the example of helping our children with their homework we often end up doing the work *for* them instead of *with* them. In these examples helping means lending a hand to pull up someone. The helper has power, while the helpee is powerless.

When we try to help people in more complex situations we realize how powerless *we* are. If you make a list of how you *tried* to help someone it might look like the following:

I tried to help him with his drug problem.

I tried to help him with his fits of depression.

I tried to help him with his drinking problem.

I tried to help him with the negative feelings he has toward his parents.

I tried to help him with his feelings toward me.

I tried to help him get a job.

I tried to help him in his career development.

I tried to help her with the conflict she feels between being a mother and being a career woman.

This list could go on and on and on. Usually, we feel most unsuccessful in trying to help the people that are closest to us. Day in and day out we feel the pain of frustration, because the more we try to help, the more helpless we feel. "If only I could get inside him, I could fix things," we tell ourselves. Or, "Why doesn't he do what I'm telling him? He just won't listen." Then we worry. Before long we blurt out our anxious self-talk in our discussions with the person that we are trying to help. We usually end up arguing. Instead of helping the other person to reduce his problems we have thrown another problem, us, on his pile of woes.

When we are making matters worse for ourselves and others by "helping," then it's time to ask ourselves, "Am I *really* helping him?" It's time to throw away the images of ourselves as the great benefactors, saviors and providers of wisdom. It's time to think of a new set of images about helping that might resemble the following:

Mountain climbers help each other scale the cliffs.

Surgeons help each other perform an operation.

Children help mothers bake a cake.

Fathers help children put together their toy trains.

Coaches help children learn how to swim.

Teachers help children learn math.

These images tell us that helping means cooperating, collaborating or working together to achieve a common objective. Simply put, *helping is the art of cooperating*. To develop an art we need to know the basic principles of the art, and then we have to be willing to apply them. The more we practice and the more we observe our practice the better we perform.

Principles of Helping

Let's highlight some of the main principles of helping:

1. People have their own vision of life.

2. People are free to commit or not commit themselves to change.

3. People are resilient. They can always bounce back after failing.

4. People have the mental abilities to change.

Let's see what each of these principles means in practice.

1. *People have their own vision of life.*

People intuitively feel that life is good and that they are valuable. When confronted with the pressures of life they can lose their vision by letting go of their concentration. People that have lost their jobs, that are on the verge of divorce, or that feel alienated from their children feel confused. Even more simple pressures, such as high school students failing a course for the first time, might feel depressed and, consequently, lose confidence in themselves. Their vision that life is good and that they are valuable, whether they succeed or fail, is buried under their confusion, frustration and depression. Helping means cooperating with the other person to get him in touch with his vision. It's like helping a builder to find the misplaced blueprints to a house that he is constructing. Until the people that we are helping get in touch with their own vision of life, no matter how clear or foggy, how sensible or strange and how reasonable or unreasonable that vision appears to us, we will feel powerless in trying to help them with their immediate problem. Some techniques that we can use to assist them to concentrate on their positive feelings about life and themselves are:

1. Suggest that they recall a past experience during a period in their lives when they felt good about themselves. Have them describe in detail their feelings, thoughts and actions and the circumstances of that experience. Ask what they felt was important in that experience.

2. Suggest that they use their imagination to describe themselves as they would like to be. Again have them pay attention to the details. Next, ask them if they have experienced in some degree the characteristics of their ideal self.

3. Ask them what in nature fills them with positive feelings. Some answers might be: the ocean, the mountains, some special place. Ask them what they are feeling and thinking when they visualize these places in nature.

4. We can do the same three exercises above and share our insights with the people that we want to help.

Helping people get in touch with their vision does not mean that they will see exactly what will happen next. It does mean that they see that they are attached to life and that they share in the goodness and creative power of life. What they will do specifically with that power is up to them. If people don't get in touch with their personal vision of life, they will expect the impossible from the people that are trying to help them.

2. *People are free to commit or not to commit themselves to change.*

No matter what we do, if someone does not want to see, does not want to understand, does not want to change, and does not want to believe that he is free to change, we are powerless to help him. Almost all people subscribe to the idea of freedom, but few *believe* that *they* are free and far fewer *believe and feel* that they are free. To be free means that we have the power to choose to act like the person that we intuitively feel we are. In the depths of our being we know that we are caring, generous and understanding. However, many people choose to believe that they are products or victims of unhealthy parental and social influences. Sometimes even the people trying to help someone believe that people are products of upbringing. Just imagine what happens when both parents and children believe that their personalities are primarily shaped by parental influence. Suppose a couple has a son addicted to drugs. The parents believing that their son is *their* product have to change *their* son or feel guilty for what *they* have produced. The son on the other hand feels that he is beyond repair because he is the product of his parents. If the son does not change, the parents will constantly and morbidly ask, "What did we do wrong?" While the parents are advising, cajoling, exhorting, threatening and monitoring their son, he is reacting negatively to their pressures by continuing his habit. On the one hand he uses his parents' guilt as an excuse for continuing his habit. "After all," he says, "If you two had brought me up better, I wouldn't be in this mess." Intuitively, however, he knows that he is responsible for his life. What he deeply wants from his parents is their respect for his freedom to make his choices and their trust in his mind to judge wisely, even though he and they know that he will make mistakes. He needs mental and emotional elbow room to get in touch with *his* vision of life. To do that he needs to be psychologically free from his parents' pressure in order to accept himself and his parents on his own terms. Parents can be truly helpful by recognizing their children's freedom of choice and by reminding their children that they are free to make their own decisions. Parents should also remind their children that true freedom is experienced when they act according to their own vision of life, that is, according to what they believe is important, good, true and worthwhile.

Believing in the power of our children to make decisions in the light of their own intuitions tests our trust in the goodness of life. Trusting the goodness of life in our children is also an act of generosity on our part. By giving them our trust we encourage them to use their freedom and intelligence wisely. We have to let go of our anxiety about being a good parent. Our self-centeredness spawns most of our worries. The less we worry about our image of being a good parent, the more we will behave like one, provided we trust and nurture our children's good judgement. If they exercise poor judgement, they will know it. They will need understanding parents to help them make better judgements the next time. The same principle of respecting our children's powers of vision and choice applies to all people that we want to help.

3. *People are resilient. They can always bounce back after failing.*

No matter how badly we act, we *can* always change to act better. Whether we *want* to change is a matter of free choice. The power to change and the reason to change are two different experiences. No matter how many good reasons we have to change our behavior, we will not change unless we *choose* to change. If we take a close look at our negative behaviors, we can see how unreasonable we are in holding on to them. Chain smokers know the reasons why they ought to change. Overeaters know the reasons why they ought to change.

Liars know the reasons why they ought to change. We all have common sense that tells us what is good for us. Yet, we *choose* to ignore what we know is true.

When people give themselves reasons to justify their negative behaviors, they are choosing not to change. Chain smokers will convince themselves that they will probably die in an accident anyway. Liars will rationalize that telling the truth will just make them vulnerable to untrustworthy people. If we do not want to change, we can always find psychological, sociological or biological reasons not to change. After awhile we begin to believe that our behaviors are the results of forces beyond our control. Then we *feel* powerless to change, but we *are* powerful. We can still choose to see ourselves as the makers of our own behaviors. Unfortunately, many people hold on to the belief that their behaviors are the results of internal and external forces beyond their control. So, they say, "I want to change, but I can't." They believe that they are powerless. They feel that they can't move themselves in the direction that they want to go. It is as if a person standing on a street corner wants to cross the street but says he can't. How do *we* help convince him to cross, when *he* wills to believe that he *can't* cross? Impossible!

Usually, when we say we *can't* change, we are talking more about our *feelings* of impotence then our *actual* power to change. We *can* always change. If we honestly want to change, we are willing to see what is required to change. Change is difficult. Change requires courage, that is, seeing the difficult choices that we ought to make and, then, directing our spiritual, physical and mental activities toward the realization of behaviors that are consistent with our vision of life. Change is not easy. Change is not comfortable. But change is always possible, if we choose to change.

4. *People have the mental abilities to change.*

As a counselor I have always believed in the resiliency and resourcefulness of the human spirit. In the final analysis people themselves identify their own problems, create their own solutions and make their own lives. I feel rage when people are ready to do whatever the therapist tells them. I feel more rage when therapists prescribe solutions for problems that the *therapist* believes that the client has. Such statements as, "I think you ought to divorce him/her"; or "Tell your boss what you really think of him," rolling glibly off the tongue of a therapist are marks of poor professional judgement. We are all too ready to shirk the responsibility of making our own decisions, and we including therapists, are all perfectly willing to tell others what they should or should not do.

We all have our own personal vision of life, and we all have the power to decide. Translating our vision into a way of living challenges our powers of creative thinking. Creative thinking is simply the mental process of coming up with new and better ways of living our vision of life. Our hopes, our values, our goals, our positive feelings toward ourselves and others make up our vision of life. Sometimes we symbolize our vision in a word, such as family, excellence, love, justice, love of God, etc. But these words that symbolize our real vision are empty, unless we discover how to fill them up with actions that are congruent with our vision. For example, our vision of life might include strong positive feelings about justice, but how do we translate that noble ideal into action at home, at work and with our neighbors? Does justice mean giving to others what they give to me? Or does justice mean that I always respect the inherent value of a person no matter what he does? When we question ourselves in this way, we are using our minds to see ourselves in relation to other people in new and different ways. We will intuitively know which actions are congruent with justice, even though we may find our new ways difficult to practice.

Usually, creative thinking is spurred on by our intuition telling us that something is not right. The experience is similar to the composer of music or the painter that feels there is something not just right about his work. Something has to be taken out or put in so that his work will be the true expression of his intuitive vision. Instead of notes and paints we use actions to express our vision of life on the canvas of time.

Living is an art. We live to make beauty, to share beauty and to enjoy beauty. We all have the power to think creatively, and we have all used this power with varying intensities during our lives. Intuitively, we know when we are not making anything, and worse, when we are making ugliness. Our intuitive awareness of the gap or the contradiction between our vision of life and our actions invites us to change. If we accept our own invitation to change, then we will think creatively to discover new ways of translating our vision into actions.

Chapter VI

Theory of Helping: Moves People Make

We all have a theory about life. Simple statements are the raw materials of our theory of life that we continually sculpt to finer points. Just the other day the owner of the hardware store around the corner applied his theory of life to the difficulties I was having in repairing a leak in the tank of the toilet bowl. Every time I tried fixing something, I created another problem. "It's one of those days, I should have stayed in bed," I said to the owner on my third trip to his store. "No! No! Never say that. We make our own days. You can still turn it around," he earnestly replied. "I guess so," I said rather feebly. "You know," he said, "Heaven and Hell are right here on earth. We make it either way." I suppose we could have talked for a few hours about his theory of life, but I did have to fix the plumbing. In a way I felt I had verified his theory when the leak was sealed.

On another occasion I called back the man that laid the wall to wall carpet in the den, because it was bulging in a particular area. After arriving at the scene he assured me that everything would turn out okay. "You know," he said, "adjusting this carpet is all part of life. Life is just a series of adjustments until we get it the way we want it."

Now it's my turn to present my theory about helping people. As I said in the last chapter, helping people is really an art of cooperating with people to assist them in clarifying and realizing their vision. This theory is grounded in the conviction that essentially we are spiritual beings with kinetic energy. That is, at our center we are powerful self-starters. Too often we think of ourselves in terms of our potential, that is, what we *could* be if... Seeing ourselves in terms of potential gives us a distorted image of ourselves. It is as if we were rockets poised on the launching pad. We wait for someone to push the button. It is far

4 7

more useful and accurate to think of ourselves primarily in terms of kinetic energy and secondarily in terms of potential. The analogy of a bird taking off fits a human being more than a rocket being blasted off. The internal kinetic energy of the bird realizes its potential to fly.

The following is a diagram of three concentric circles to show the relationship among body, psyche and spirit.

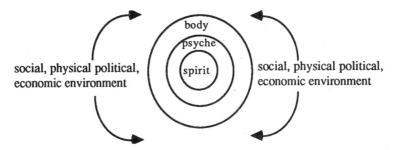

The spiritual dimension is the source of our vision, freedom, resiliency and creativity. It is not necessarily religious, that is, consciously related to a Supreme Being, although that is one of its choices. Let's take an example of depression to see how this part of the theory works in practice. Suppose John feels depressed. He says that he is failing in his work and his relationships. Drinking is the means he uses to forget the image that he has of himself as a worthless person. Suppose we believe that the depression has infested *all* of John's being. Imagine a circle representing his being completely filled with depression.

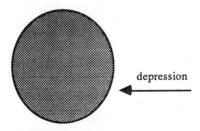

Is there any way for the circle to rid itself of depression? If all of John is saturated with depression, he cannot change himself. If he can't empty himself of his depression, someone will have to do it for him. If this line of thinking is correct, John will always have to depend on someone to rescue him from his depression.

An alternative way of visualizing John's depression is to see it affecting the outer two circles of his being.

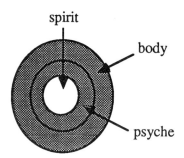

The spiritual dimension of our being never gets depressed. Depression is a word that we use to describe ourselves psychologically and physically. In this alternative image John is free from depression at the center of his being. His spiritual activities of intuition and self reflection are minimally operative, yet they function enough to make him aware of his depression in the psychological and physical dimensions of his being.

Many times I have asked people experiencing depression to visualize the center of their being. They can do this exercise after they have gotten in touch with positive memories of themselves and the central values of their lives. Most people use some image of light to describe their center. In other words they are saying that *essentially* they are depression-free. The next step is to find out how to use the light and energy to disperse the depression in their physical and psychological dimensions. After a person recognizes his center of light and energy, we can be helpful.

The spiritual center of every human being is whole, entire, healthy, free, creative, reflective and intuitive. There is no such thing as a sick spirit. There is, however, the reality of a despairing spirit. At the center of our being we make the ultimate choice to live or not live, to be or not be and to see or not see. Despair is far beyond depression. When depressed we *feel* like nothing. When despairing we *choose* to be nothing. In despair we chose not to reflect, not to intuit, not to decide, not to think creatively and not to accept our connection to life. As long as someone had not despaired, we can be helpful.

Helping People Get in Touch With Their Tendencies

In the theory of helping people that I am proposing, the *idea of movement is central*. Instead of seeing ourselves in roles, such as parents, spouses, teachers, managers, etc, or in ego states, such as parent, adult and child, we can see ourselves as moving beings, that is we tend toward one direction or another. In everyday language we describe ourselves as moving beings by saying we are on our way up, we are sinking, or we are moving along. By identifying our tendencies we will be able to see more clearly the direction in which we are moving. The following Human Tendencies Profile can act as a compass that tells us where we are and where we are headed.

Human Tendencies Profile

Irrational	Rational	Supra-Rational
confusion	order	vision
dependence	control	freedom
rebellion	system	change
skepticism	certainty	creativity
(move down toward)	(move toward)	(move up toward)
self-destruction	self-profit	making our world

Irrational Tendencies

A tendency is a type of movement that we experience in ourselves. The three categories of movement are irrational, rational and supra-rational. Irrational types of movement tend toward self-destruction. Rational types of movement tend toward self-profit. Supra-rational types of movement tend toward world-making. Each tendency is a movement made up of emotions, behaviors and thinking. For example, when we say that we feel confused, we usually experience anxiety, behave erratically and think in some special illogical way. Confusion is a movement that points us in the direction toward the next irrational tendency, dependence. If we are confused in a relationship, we often depend on someone else to tell us what to do. We might feel a lack of confidence in our own judgement, and we think that we can't clarify our own thinking. Consequently, we are ready to ask for and accept the opinions of other people. If their advice does not work for us, we usually rebel against the people that are trying to help us. Skepticism follows rebellion. We lose trust in ourselves and others. These irrational tendencies follow one after the other and move us toward self-destruction in a downward movement.

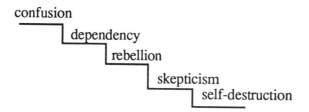

confusion
dependency
rebellion
skepticism
self-destruction

Rational Tendencies

Our rational tendencies move us along on a level plain. The first rational tendency is order. We always want some order in our personal lives, our relationships, our work and our physical environment. Without order we feel that we are losing control. For example, if the kitchen is disorganized, pots helter-skelter, food lying around, pilot lights out, dirty dishes in the sink and a leaky faucet, we find it difficult to put a meal together. We have to get things in order before we can get control of the kitchen. We tend to put things and ourselves in patterns and sequences for some purpose. We might arrange our furniture in a certain pattern for a practical reason, such as making it easy for people to talk to one another or to watch TV.

Control usually follows order. If we put order in our thinking when making a decision, we usually experience greater control over our anxiety. In the case of making a decision putting order in our thinking means to do step-by-step thinking that will lead us to the realization of what is most important to us. If we are making a career decision, we sort out what is most important to us in our work, e.g. money, the enjoyment of the work itself, the opportunity to learn and to become more proficient, etc. Then, we look at our skills, interests and past performance to see which position will match us at this time. As we think in an orderly way, we feel a sense of power and mastery. We feel that we are directing ourselves.

The first two tendencies of order and control are followed by system, certainty and self-profit. The tendency for system means that we try to relate the different aspects of our lives harmoniously. The same decision-making process that we used for career development, we can also use for parent development and spouse development. However, all three are now connected, so that what we do in one area will have an effect on another area.

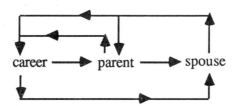

career ⟶ parent ⟶ spouse

If we have achieved some balance in the system, then we experience the next tendency of certainty or at least a measure of certainty. The tendency of certainty moves us to do much testing-thinking . We probe ourselves and we probe others to make sure that everything is going okay. While at work we might call home to find out if Johnny is doing his homework. Then, when we are at home we might call a colleague to exchange ideas about a project. We are always trying to get "it"–life–all together, so that we will feel secure. All of these rational tendencies lead us to a sense of self-profit, that is, a sense of well-being, worth and usefulness.

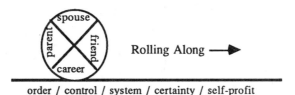

Rolling Along ⟶

order / control / system / certainty / self-profit

Supra-rational Tendencies

Our supra-rational tendencies move us toward *making* our world, whereas the rational tendencies direct us to *manage* life. The supra-rational tendencies inspire us to make a better world in which to live. Vision, the first supra-rational tendency, is the experience of being in touch with the goodness and beauty of life within our own being through the power of intuition. In the tendency of vision we also use our intellect, sensations, emotions and creative imagination to symbolize the now fullness of life and to prefigure its future forms. For example, in the tendency of vision we may experience the essential unity of life even though in the psycho-social dimension of our lives we feel fragmented. In our vision we can see the unity that we can make if we choose to do so.

Freedom which is the power to choose to actualize the possibilities that we see is the second supra-rational tendency. We are so free that we can even choose to close our eyes to our internal vision. Very often we turn our backs on our freedom out of fear or laziness. We simply do not want the responsibility for making our life and our world. It's much easier to depend on someone else to tell us what to do or to satisfy our needs. When we are not satisfied, we can always blame someone else for our miserable life. To escape freedom is to run into the jaws of disaster. If we do not choose to make our world of work and our world of relationships, we will find ourselves trapped in someone else's irrational world.

Change is the next supra-rational tendency. Change is supra-rational because it is based on our vision. History is full of examples of people who turned their behaviors and ways of thinking around a hundred and eighty degrees. We might know more common examples of change such as people that stopped drinking and smoking. The religious term for such a change is conversion, which means to turn around. In change we remember the goodness of life that we were in touch with intuitively. At times we find ourselves drifting away from that vision. Then, we turn around and go back to our vision. Reformed alcoholics are good examples of change. All the best rational arguments in the world cannot change an alcoholic. Change comes when the alcoholic *sees* something or someone of value to him.

The tendency of creativity follows change. In the tendency of creativity we think in order to discover ways of translating our vision of life into particular actions. For example, in our vision of love we may have symbolized the dynamic generosity of love with a human heart. Holding nothing for itself the heart pumps the blood of life to the rest of the body. This symbol excites our creative imagination to think of generous actions that will construct our world of love. Creativity is the work of our subjective mind inspired by our intuitive grasp of life by which we enlarge the objective goodness and beauty of our world. All our supra-rational tendencies cooperate to make a beautiful internal and external world.

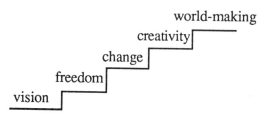

According to the theory, with which we can agree or disagree based on our own experiences, our supra-rational tendencies ought to guide our rational tendencies. The order in our life, that is, our patterns of behaviors and our basic beliefs guiding our thinking ought to be the rational expression of our personal and intuitive vision of life. For example, we trust people because we *believe* that they are trustworthy even though we have plenty of evidence to say that people are not always trustworthy. Even if we have been cheated by people, our vision of the ultimate goodness of life in people will still guide our thinking and behavior. According to statistical and empirical evidence and our own experience, we can never be sure who is trustworthy and who is not. Yet we choose to follow our vision that people are trustworthy, and we continue to order our rational thinking according to that vision. If we choose not to follow our supra-rational tendencies, then our rational tendencies will be guided by our irrational tendencies. Skepticism will shape our beliefs in our dealings with people. "Don't trust anyone until they have proven themselves beyond doubt," will be the principle directing our thinking and behaviors. When our rational tendencies are guided by our irrational tendencies we become more neurotic each day.

In helping people we are cooperating with them to minimize the pull of their irrational tendencies on their rational tendencies and to maximize the influence of their supra-rational tendencies over their rational tendencies.

minimize influence	*maximize interaction*	
Irrational	Rational	Supra-Rational
confusion	order	vision
dependence	control	freedom
rebellion	system	change
skepticism	certainty	creativity
(move down toward)	(move toward)	(move up toward)
self-destruction	self-profit	making our world

Too often we use our rational tendencies to justify our irrational tendencies that are dragging us to self-destruction. Intuitively we know that rational tendencies ought to be at the service of our vision and ought not to be catering to our confusion, dependence, rebellion and skepticism. Now that we are clear about *what* we want to do, let's find out *how* to do it.

Chapter VII

Helping Skills

Cicero, the Roman orator-philosopher, wrote that friendship is based on virtue. Virtue means strengths of character that we are in the habit of using. Patience is one of the most important virtues in helping someone. Patience means being there, listening, respecting and waiting to hear something positive to build on. To help someone means to cooperate at the pace of the helpee. Sometimes we may see what the real issue is, but the person that we are helping doesn't see it. For example, an alcoholic never sees himself as an alcoholic. He sees problems out there, all around him, that have to be solved. For him, a new job, a raise in salary, getting away from his in-laws, or moving to another state, would bring harmony into his life. "Drinking? That's not a problem," he curtly says. Even if he stops drinking, he still has to face himself. He still has to give up the belief that he is the victim of all the problems out there. While trying to help people who are using reason to build defenses around their irrational tendencies, we can easily become frustrated. However, by patiently dialoguing about experiences related to their supra-rational tendencies we are fanning the embers of their intuition and ultimate choice. If we and they stay at the positive dialogue long enough, the internal flames of life will burst forth. The people that we are helping will begin to see.

Skill one: Listening

Listening is one of the most important skills in helping anyone: children, spouses, friends, relatives, colleagues, etc. No one likes to be told what to do, and most of all no one likes to be analyzed. Listening is the best skill to help people get in touch with their vision. Listening is more than hearing. To listen means to put ourselves in the skin of the other person so that we can, as much as possible, feel, sense and think as the other person is feeling, sensing and thinking. To listen means to leave behind our ego, our world and our critical judgements, so that we are there one-hundred percent for the other person.

If we listen well, we can reflect to the person what he is thinking, feeling and doing in a particular situation. For example, suppose our teenage daughter comes home and says, "The teachers in that school are unfair and inconsiderate." We could reply by asking, "What happened?" or "What do you mean?" On the other hand, if we are listening, that is, if we are experiencing the world of our child at that moment, we will feel her hurt, which may be in the form of anger, frustration or embarrassment. An accurate and understanding reply would be, "You feel very angry and annoyed at your teachers right now." This statement says, "I am listening to you, I understand what you are feeling now, and I'm responding to you." The goal of listening is to respond to the person. Remember, people can solve their own problems once they get in touch with their supra-rational tendencies. If we start to ask questions about how the teachers were unfair and inconsiderate, we might end up taking the side of the teachers. Then, we will be perceived by our child as unfair, and even if the teachers were unfair, we can't go down to the school and make them fair.

Reflecting accurately the feelings that someone has toward someone or something is a skill that we can develop. To develop the skill we have to concentrate on the principles that we listed in Chapter One: 1) people have their own vision of life; 2) people are free to commit or not to commit themselves to change; 3) people are resilient; 4) people can think creatively.

The following are some attitudes that prevent listening:

--"I've had that experience and this is what I did." Translation: "I don't know how to fix that."

--"Time will take care of that." Translation: "Don't bother me with your silly problems."

--"Yeah... I know. Teachers are always doing crazy things." Translation: "I'm not like that. I'm on your side."

--"Let's find the cause of this problem." Translation: "Let's solve this problem once and for all." And sometimes we add, "I'm tired of your complaints."

Any attitude that gets in the way of *responding to the person* is not useful in helping someone, no matter how good our intentions are. To help is to cooperate, that is, to work *with* people to actualize *their* vision. If they are not in touch with their vision, then helping means using skills that will introduce intuition and self-reflection into the dialogue so that they will feel challenged to envision what they feel is truly important to them.

The simple skill of reflecting a person's feelings about someone or something is not difficult at all. The difficulty in applying the skill effectively lies within ourselves. The successful application of the skill is more often a matter of virtue than a question of proficiency. To listen means to will to forget ourselves, our own problems, our own emotions, and our own tendency to control everything and everyone. To listen means to will to love, that is, to be there unselfishly for the other, not because he is *our* son, *our* father,*our* client, *our* friend, or *our* student. We choose to be there for the other person simply because the other *person* is there, and the other person is inviting us informally into *his* world. Keep in mind the other person *can* take care of himself. We are invited to care *with* him about himself.

Skill two: Spotting defenses

Our weak psyche defends itself against the penetrating spiritual power of self-reflection and the confronting spiritual power of ultimate choice. Since we do not handle well the unsettling emotions of anxiety and frustration when faced with our own inadequacies, we project them onto someone else. We see in others what we will not face in ourselves. Then, we point the finger of condemnation at them. Constant negative criticism of other people is a clue that a person is probably defending his psychological ego from the nagging questions of his spirit. We cannot dim the light of our spirit, so we protect our ego from its penetrating rays by weaving a blanket of defenses over it.

Statements such as:

"He doesn't care about me."

"I'm not recognized in this company."

"She doesn't try to understand my children."

are cover-ups for:

"I don't care about him."

"I don't recognize anybody in this company."

"I don't try to understand my children."

If we were to admit to ourselves our own inadequacies and ill feelings toward others, we might feel confused about ourselves. We would then use our rational and supra-rational tendencies to get out of our confusion. Instead, we more often protect ourselves from admitting our own confusion by projecting our inadequacies toward others. By imagining our faults in other people we protect ourselves from a critical assessment of our own behaviors. If people criticize us for a defect that we do not see in ourselves because we are too busy projecting it toward others, we become rebellious and skeptical toward them.

Two other defense mechanisms that we use together are *denial and rationalization.* When caught in a lie by his parents a teenager might say, "I'm not lying. I didn't buy the drugs. I was just the middleman for my friend. You know... sometimes you have to do things for friends that you really don't want to do." We use denial and rationalization to avoid confusion, but in the end we become more confused. Suppose the teenager told the truth. "Yes, I bought the drugs. It was a wrong thing to do." He would feel confused about his relationship with his parents. He let them down. He would also feel guilty and embarrassed. He defends himself by not facing the truth. This way he feels in control rather than confused.

When helping people we might be keenly aware that the person is using defense mechanisms. It is not helpful to destroy these protective ways of thinking and behaving. They have to be dismantled from the inside by the person himself. People will dismantle them when they are in touch with their supra-rational tendencies. Our task is to cooperate with them in using their spiritual powers of self-reflection, intuition, ultimate choice and creative thinking in order to help them get in touch with their personal vision of life. For example, if someone says, "He doesn't care about me," we might respond by saying, "You feel disappointed because you feel that he doesn't care about you." The key words in the response are: "Because *you feel...*" The person might respond by saying, "Yeah, I feel that he ought to be more considerate." Our response might be, "You feel that a caring person is a considerate person." By proceeding this way the person is getting in touch with his vision of a caring person and away from his criticisms of another person. At some point in the dialogue he will realize that a caring person is not a critical and whining person. He will be ready to take a look at his own behavior in the light of his personal vision of a caring person.

If our attitude toward people is non-judgmental, that is, neither condoning nor condemning, people will feel free from anxiety and free to examine their own attitudes as they dialogue with us. In a short period of time they will get in touch with their deep intuitions about goodness, beauty, wonder and the mystery of life. From the vantage point of their supra-rational tendencies of vision and freedom they will see that it is time to change. Instead of psychologically projecting their inadequacies toward others, they will confront their weaknesses and see them as challenges to develop their psychological dimension creatively. For example, they will replace destructive criticism of others with a realistic assessment of self and others. Then they will think creatively to realize the central values of their personal vision of life.

Skill three: Spotlighting contradictions

If we listen well, we will see the contradictions in the life of the person that we are trying to help. Usually, the contradiction is the opposition between what the helpee deeply and intuitively sees and what he does and how he thinks. The following are some general types of contradictions:

Intuitively		Thinking	Behavior
I see that I am good.	But	I doubt my worth.	I'm afraid to fail so I live a safe routine.
I see that I am free.	But	I believe I'm trapped.	I don't try to change anything.
I see that I can creatively do new things.	But	I believe I'm only an average person.	I behave with excessive caution.

Some of the emotions that he might experience while holding on to his contradictions are: frustration, anger, neurotic guilt, neurotic anxiety, depression, resentment and hatred. After holding on to his contradictions for a long time, he becomes tired. This kind of tiredness is similar to the kind that we experience when pushing a car stuck in a ditch. We are pushing one way, and some unknown force is blocking our efforts. We can push some more or find out what is blocking the wheels. In life the blocking force is the *BUT* between our intuition and thinking. When listening to people we often hear something like, "I'd like to change, *but...*" Then, we hear all *"their"* rational thoughts supporting their irrational tendencies of confusion, dependence, rebellion and skepticism. Their thinking contradicts their supra-rational tendencies of vision, freedom, change and creativity. As soon as we hear a specific case of one of these general types of contradictions, such as "Yeah...deep down I know that someone can love me and I can love someone, *but* let's face it, I haven't been successful at love. No! No! No more commitment for me! I want to be free," then it's time to kick the *BUT* out of the contradiction. We can reflect the statement with a little modification and say, "You are lovable, *AND* you can love, *AND* you believe that up to now you haven't realized the love that you feel is possible." By using *AND* we are presenting the same content in the form of a challenge. If the person holds on to the *AND*, he will be talking to himself in a hopeful and realistic way. There is always a gap, not a real contradiction, between what we see intuitively and what we have done until now. If we help someone clarify conceptually their intuitions, they will experience more challenges and fewer contradictions. As soon as life is experienced as a challenge instead of a contradiction by the people that we are helping, the negative emotions of frustration, fear and anger, will yield to hope, confidence, enthusiasm and courage.

The strategy of helping

Since we all experience the full range of human tendencies—irrational, rational, supra-rational—we experience the interplay of our own tendencies and those of the persons that we are helping when we are dialoguing with them. Suppose we are talking with someone who is very confused. Let us suppose that we are concerned about helping the person so that he will experience order and control in his life. *He* is in touch with his irrational tendencies (**I**), and *we* are in touch with our rational tendencies (**R**). Our conversation can be symbolized by **I-R**. On the surface the **I-R** relationship is clear. However, we have to be equally clear about the direction of our conversation that is represented by a denominator. The tendencies in the denominator of our human interactions can be conscious or unconscious. It is always best for both parties to be aware of all tendencies underlying their interactions. In the first example we will see that the common denominator is an irrational tendency that is operating unconsciously.

If the common denominator is I, then the helper is not helping. The conversation in an **I-R/I** might be:

I (helpee): I'm so confused about myself, my job and my marriage.
R (helper): Don't worry. You can *depend* on me to take care of you.
I (helpee): What do you mean?
R (helper): If you rely on me and follow my way of doing things you will get control of your life.
I (helpee): Tell me what to do.

In this conversation the common denominator is the irrational tendency of dependency. The confused person is willing to be dependent in order to get rid of his confusion. The false helper can "help" only if the confused person depends on him. The helper is really dependent on the confused person to remain dependent on the helper. This type of relationship can be very destructive for both parties.

The other combination **I-R/R** is a relationship in which the psychological contract says that we are aiming to build a rational basis in our conversation. Then we can move from an **I-R/R** combination to an **R-R/R** combination. From the **R-R** combination we can introduce an **S**, that is, our supra-rational tendencies. Then, we can have the two following combinations.

R-S/R   or   **R-S/S**

An **I-R/R** conversation might be:

> I (helpee): I'm confused about what career I ought to go into.
> R (helper): What are you interested in?
> I (helpee): Really, outdoor life...nature.
> R (helper): What are you good at in school?
> I (helpee): I do well in science.
> R (helper): Maybe you could research the Dictionary of Occupational Titles to get some idea of the different outdoor occupations using science.

In this conversation "R" is educating "I" in the process of learning about himself and work, so that "I" can put order in his own life.

An **R-S/R** conversation might be:

> R (helpee): I'm pretty clear about what I'm good at and what careers I would be successful at, but I wonder which one I ought to choose.
> S (helper): What and who are most important to you?
> R (helpee): My wife, who is expecting, is most important; then, our whole family. Doing something socially worthwhile is also important.

In this conversation the helper, "S" is in touch with the supra-rational tendency of vision. The helpee, "R" is trying to decide on a career that will suit him. The helper is raising questions about personal values so that the helpee's career choice will be guided by his own values. The helpee wants to choose a career that will be to his self-profit, but as we saw above true self-profit is experienced when our rational tendencies are guided by our supra-rational tendency of vision.

Once the career decision is made, then an **R-R/R** conversation might take place.

> R (helpee): I'm clear about my career goal. I want to be a marine biologist. I'm wondering which program I might apply for?
>
> R.(helper): Let's get the information on the universities offering that program. We will find out which one suits you best.

In this interchange the *helpee* is using *his* reason to achieve his goal of being an effective helper.

An **R-S/S** conversation is one in which the helpee, "**R**," is concerned about how his rational choice, in this case becoming a marine biologist, will contribute to making a better world. The helper, "**S**," is playing the role of the helpee's supra-rational tendencies to bring to light how the helpee's tendencies of vision, freedom, change and creativity can be used in his vocational choice in order to make a better world.

The following are some of the usual interpersonal interactions of tendencies that we might experience when we are tying to help someone. *The helper's response determines the type of tendency in the denominator*. Either the helpee or the helper or both will verbalize the tendency in the denominator when both persons are dialoguing. If the tendency in the denominator remains unconscious to both the helpee and helper, the helping process is impaired

$$\frac{\text{I - I}}{\text{I}}$$ I (helpee): I'm confused.   I (helper): I'm confused.
     I: No hope

$$\frac{\text{I - R}}{\text{I}}$$ I (helpee): I can't trust anyone.   R (helper): Facts and history support your idea.
     I: We can't even trust each other.

$$\frac{\text{I - R}}{\text{R}}$$ I (helpee): I can't live without you.   R (helper): Were you able to live before you knew me?
     R: It might be painful but we can live productively without each other.

R - R
R

R (helpee): We don't agree   R (helper): Right, let's
 on how to raise children   examine our differences.
R: We *can* find principles that
we both agree on.

R - S
R

R (helpee): I'm losing   S (helper): Maybe it's time
 control of my life.   see what's important to you.
R: If I put my thinking in order according
to my values, I'll get control.

I - S
S

I (helpee): I'm trapped in   S (helper): Who chose the
 this relationship.   trap?
S: I *feel* trapped, but I see that I *am* free.

R - S
S

R (helpee): Now that I have   S (helper): Maybe it's time to
 it all, what will I do?   act creatively.
S: Living is making, not just having.

S - S
S

S (helpee): Love is the most   S (helper): What does love
 important thing in my life.   mean to you?
S: By sharing our vision we are cooperating
to discover ways to make a beautiful world.

The strategy of the helper is to dialogue in word and/or action in such a way to excite the rational and supra-rational tendencies of the helpee.

First move:	Listen in a non-judgmental way to create an atmosphere of trust and self-acceptance in which the helpee feels free to use his powers of intuition, self-reflection, ultimate choice, and creativity.
Second move:	Spot defenses preventing the helpee from accepting his inadequacies and from owning his emotions and actions.
Third move:	Spotlight the contradictions so that the helpee sees the interplay between his irrational and rational or supra-rational tendencies.
Fourth move:	Label the common denominator, that is, the direction of the dialogue toward the

development of a specific rational and /or
supra-rational tendency.

Remember, helping is the art of cooperating. The art practiced at its
best yields the following relationship among people: **S-S/S**. In this
relationship cooperating is a way of living in which people share their
vision of life and support each other in making a world according to
that vision.

If we are helping someone over a long period of time, for example,
our children, then we will experience most of the combinations of
tendencies listed above. The most frequently experienced combinations in helping people develop are **I-R/R** and **I-S/S**.

The **I-R/I** is a deceptive combination. We have to guard ourselves
against it, particularly when helping children develop. Children are
naturally dependent on adults for food, clothing, shelter, and feeling
of belonging and learning. However, children are naturally moving
toward independence. Intuitively, they know when that movement is
being blocked by dominating and possessive parents. They also intuitively know when they themselves are impeding their own movement, such as playing on their parents' false sense of guilt in order to
be pampered by them. When children reach their teens, they know that
they are now responsible for their own thinking and learning.
Sometimes their new found mental independence might take the form
of rebellion. Parents have to be careful in talking with teenagers so
that they avoid the **I-R/I** trap.

<u>I: teenage rebellion   R: parental control</u>
I: mutual rebellion and
skepticism (lack of trust)

In listing the combinations of tendencies that we experience in relationships, I left out the following one: **I-S/I**. It's difficult to imagine
an irrational common denominator between a helper in touch with
supra-rational tendencies and a helpee struggling with his irrational
tendencies. It seems that this combination **I-S/I** happens more in religion and national ideologies than in any other area of life. The helpee
might be on his way to self-destruction, either physical and/or mental,
and the "helper" saves him from eternal perdition. The helpee in this
scenario trades in the irrational tendency of skepticism for the irrational tendency of dependence. The "savior" acting out of a vision of
eternal salvation depends on the irrational tendencies of people in
order for him to be a savior with a small "s." True religion would
inspire a **I-S/S** combination. True religious conversion is

accompanied by a feeling of freedom, creativity and a belief in the power of one's own mind.

In the following chapters we will explain how the **I-R/R, I-S/S** and **I-R/I** combinations operate and what moves so that we as helpers can make to assist the helpee in responding to his R and S tendencies. We will also explain ways of guarding ourselves against being trapped by our own irrational tendencies when we feel frustrated in tying to help someone.

The Two Basic Moves to Help Someone.

We can help someone by:

1. Guiding them first toward their rational tendency of order and then toward their supra-rational tendency of vision.

or

2. Guiding them first toward their supra-rational tendency of vision and then toward their rational tendency of order.

The option that we as helpers exercise will depend on the condition of the helpee. Although there are people that think logically, nevertheless they are confused because they are not in touch with their vision. On the other hand there are people that are somewhat intuitively in touch with their vision of life, but their chaotic thinking aborts the actualization of their vision.

Part Two

STRATEGIES FOR HELPING PEOPLE EXPERIENCING STRONG IRRATIONAL TENDENCIES

Chapter VIII

Helping The Confused Person

—"I'm confused. I just don't know what to do with this relationship."

—"I don't know what to do about my kids."

—"Should I stay in this job or should I move on. One day I'm moving and the next day I'm staying."

—"I thought I had life figured out. Now I seem to be losing control."

Statements such as these tell us that the people whom we are tying to help are wandering and drifting. Usually they are indecisive. If they do make a decision, it is an impulsive move made out of frustration and anxiety. They just want to stop feeling confused. We've all experienced that feeling of confusion in some degree. It's like wandering in the desert, getting lost in the forest or aimlessly rowing in a lifeboat in the middle of the ocean. When we have reached the panic point, we pick a direction and move. We don't know where we are going, but the feeling of being on the way to somewhere is better than the feeling of going around in circles. As we mentioned before, the movement of confusion, and the movement of all our tendencies, is made up of emotions, behaviors and ways of thinking. Confusion can consist of any combination of the following:

EMOTIONS:
anxiety, frustration, apprehension, fear, diffidence (lack of confidence).

BEHAVIORS:
> erratic, jumping from one thing to another, impulsive moves, searching for a resting place, looking for someone to lean on, using caustic, complaining and blaming language.

WAYS OF THINKING:
> endlessly weighing possibilities; thinking about the past in "if only..." terms, e.g., "if only I had met the right person; if only I had chosen a different job," etc.; expecting someone or some event to save me; excessive day dreaming; always thinking about what other people are thinking of me; judging my self-worth according to past performance.

All the emotions, behaviors and ways of thinking are not listed here, but we have enough information to help someone who says, "I'm confused." Before continuing let's look at all the tendencies again in a diagram that will give us a sense of movement.

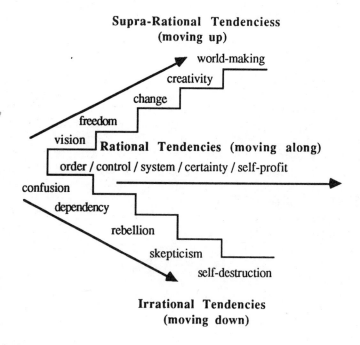

Supra-Rational Tendenciess
(moving up)

world-making
creativity
change
freedom
vision   **Rational Tendencies (moving along)**
order / control / system / certainty / self-profit
confusion
dependency
rebellion
skepticism
self-destruction

Irrational Tendencies
(moving down)

When someone says "I'm confused about...," we know that they are one step down from the **R** tendency of order. If we observe them carefully, we will be able to identify some of their behaviors and emotions associated with confusion. We know that the confused person is moving away from order and control and is on his way down to self-destruction. Usually, the erratic behavior of the confused person is evident to us. "Nothing that he does or says makes sense," we tell ourselves. Then, we ask ourselves, "How did he get that way?" The helpee is probably asking himself the same question, "How did *I* get this way?"

At this point he is fabricating excuses that will explain his chaotic life. Usually, he will find plenty of "reasons" outside himself. There is no doubt that we have all suffered negative experiences at the hands of someone else's neglect or down right rottenness. Probably the worst experience that we can imagine is incest suffered by a child over a long period of time. Obviously, incest will severely *damage* a person's sexual identity, self-esteem, self-worth, value system, sense of trust and many other aspects of the person's psychological and physical dimensions. As insidious as violent incest is, it will *damage*, but it cannot *destroy* the person. Remember, the spiritual dimension of a person cannot be violated from the outside. Many people that suffered from incest intuitively know what they had to do for themselves to *regain* a feeling of psychological self-worth. All along they intuitively knew that their value was "*there.*" "There" in this sense means deep within themselves at the center of their being. Their challenge was to respond to their intuition and courageously work at rehabilitating their severely wounded psychological dimension. To achieve this kind of psychological renewal is a long and arduous task. I am using incest to show that no matter *what* happens to us, no matter *when* it happens to us, and no matter *by whom* it happens to us, we can still undo the psychological confusion that has its start from some external source. However, once we are aware of our own confusion, then *we* are the cause of keeping it or undoing it. Some other external sources of confusion might be:

--"I got fired. Why? I don't know."

--"My kid is on drugs. What did I do wrong?"

--"The other night she told me our relationship was over."

--"Why do my parents treat me this way? I've done everything to please them."

--"I lived by the book. I did everything I was supposed to do. Why aren't things working out the way they are supposed to? My marriage is falling apart. I'm falling apart. My kids are drifting away."

We can use two strategies to help the confused person.

Strategy one: Moving from confusion to order.

While listening to someone expressing his confusion, we have to keep our mind on his behaviors and his thinking. We can draw into the open someone's thinking by asking him to tell us what they are saying to themselves when they are behaving erratically. The point in having someone say out loud what they are saying over and over to themselves internally is to discover the disorder in their thinking. The following are some examples:

Scenario 1:

Seventeen year-old son: You and Mom have me going in circles. You want me to be responsible, but you don't trust my judgement.

Father: You feel confused about what we expect from you.

Son: Yeah!

Father: When you feel that way, I mean confused, what are you saying to yourself?

Son: I'm saying, I can't win. When I do what I think is best I lose with my parents. When I do what they think is best I lose with myself.

Father: It seems that you believe that all your decisions should get our approval.

Son: Yeah!

Father: Is that a reasonable belief? Do you approve all the decisions we make?

Son: Yes and no. I mean, YES, I think it's reasonable to expect your approval, and NO, I don't go along with all your decisions.

Father: So, its reasonable for *you* not to always go along with *our* decisions, but it is not reasonable for *us* not to always go along with *your* decisions.

Son: I guess I'm being unreasonable. Maybe it's reasonable to expect a difference of opinion.

Father: Maybe you wouldn't feel confused if you *expected* us to disagree with you at times.

Scenario 2:

Colleague-Friend (helpee): I've been with this company for fourteen years now, and I haven't got the promotions that I wanted. I'm beginning to feel like part of the furniture around here. I had a clear idea of myself when I started here, but now I'm doubting myself.

Colleague-Friend (helper): You haven't been promoted and you feel upset with yourself.

Colleague-Friend (helpee): Let's face it. I've been passed over. I feel like a round peg trying to fit in a square. The way I feel about myself is now affecting my work. I have to make a move. I'm going in circles, and I've got to get out of this.

Colleague-friend (helper): It seems that the feelings you have about yourself depend on whether you are promoted. Suppose the boss promoted you today, would you feel better about yourself?

Colleague-Friend:(helpee): I guess so.

Colleague-Friend (helper): It seems that the boss has the power to confuse you or unconfuse you about yourself. Does that seem reasonable?

Colleague-Friend (helpee): No, it's not reasonable. I guess I feel confused because I'm not in touch with my true feeings about myself. I'm confusing the feelings I have about not being promoted with the honest feelings I have about myself.

In both of these cases the helper sees from the beginning that irrational thinking in the form of unreasonable assumptions, expectations and/or beliefs is holding the helpee in his confusion. The helper needs to use the skill of *leading* the helpee to become aware of his irrational thinking without directly telling the helpee that he has erroneous assumptions or unreasonable expectations.

The following are some questions that the helper can ask himself while dialoguing with the helpee.

Does the helpee place the cause of his confusion outside of himself in someone or some event?

Does the helpee equate his self-worth with his performance as a parent, spouse and/or professional?

Does the helpee do inappropriate comparative thinking, for example comparing his measure of happiness, prestige and possessions with his neighbors' and colleagues' successes in those areas?

If the answer is "yes" to any one of the above, then the helper ought to articulate and go along with the irrational assumption of the helpee in order to show how that assumption leads the helpee to absurd consequences. For example, if self-worth is equated with performance, we will have to conclude that old people, the handicapped and the mentally ill are marginal human beings.

The basic idea behind strategy one, moving from confusion to order, is to help the confused person to think about *how*, not what, but HOW, he is thinking. The following chart identifies the components of this strategy.

Self Statements	Emotions	Behaviors	Assumptions	Expectations	Values
I'm angry as hell, I've been here a long time and I did not get a promotion I think I'm loosing it.	Anger Frustration	Passive-aggressive foot dragging, complaining	My value depends on getting a promotion	I expect my career to go downhill if I don't get promoted.	Excellence Achievement
Self Statements	Emotions	Behaviors	Assumptions	Expectations	Values

Identify the minus and plus items in the chart. Change the minus items to plus items. If the emotions are minus such as anger and frustration in our example, then check the assumptions and expectations first. If the assumptions and the expectations are unreasonable, change them so that they are reasonable. Do you need to add new values? Then change the self-statement based on your new assumption. As you talk to yourself now, what emotion are you experiencing and what new behaviors will you choose?

After the helpee has identified the minus items keeping him in his confusion and has made the necessary changes in his assumptions, expectations and ways of thinking, such as thinking in more specific terms rather than generalizing; thinking of himself as a unique being rather than comparing himself to others; distinguishing his unique value from his imperfect performance; and thinking of himself as a cause rather than an effect, then we are ready for strategy two, moving from confusion to vision back to order.

Strategy two: Moving from confusion to vision to order.

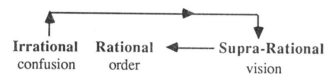

Irrational **Rational** ◄——— **Supra-Rational**
confusion   order   vision

In the self-statement chart above the helpee identified what was important to him by listing his values. For example, in the dialogue between the father and son, the son is valuing his love for his parents, and at the same time he values his power to make his own decisions. The father can help his son focus on his supra-rational tendency of vision by reflecting his son's own sense of valuing. The dialogue might go like:

Son: I can't seem to win with you. You want me to be responsible, but you don't trust my judgment.

Father: You value your own judgement, and at the same time you are concerned about how your decisions will affect us.

Son: Yeah. Making my own decisions is important to me and...

Father: And your mother and I are important to you.

Son: But who comes first?

Father: Well...what does your best insight tell you?

Son: I know you and Mom deeply care for me, and I want to do my best for you.

Father: So I think you're saying that we love you and you love us. We're concerned about what you

Son:

> do because we love you, and you're concerned
> about our reactions because you love us.
> That's right, my love for you is important, and
> making my own decisions is important. Some-
> how I have to keep them together.

Generally speaking our real dialogues are not as short and as compact as the ones I have presented. However, if we keep in mind that irrational thinking and lack of concentration on what we truly value are the two major internal sources of confusion, we can quickly help someone by leading him to identify his particular type of irrational thinking and focus on his central but forgotten value. Frequently, people are confused because they experience a conflict of values. For example, we value our career *and* our family. If we spend a good deal of time doing what our career requires, then we might feel guilty about not spending enough time with our family. We can be in touch with our supra-rational tendency of vision, but when we try to translate our values into actions we slip into irrational thinking. We might say to ourselves something like: "I can't please everyone. If I don't put in extra time at work, I'll never get the approval of my boss and that means no promotion. If I do put in the time at work I'll lose the approval of my husband/wife and children." Let me put those statements in an IRS combination.

$$\frac{S - I}{I} \quad \frac{\begin{array}{ll} \textbf{S} \text{ I value my career} & \textbf{I} \text{ I can't please both} \\ \text{and family} & \text{(either/or thinking)} \end{array}}{\begin{array}{l} \textbf{I} \text{ I need the approval of both boss and} \\ \text{family (dependency). I'm confused.} \end{array}}$$

To eliminate the confusion in the denominator, we have to get rid of the I (either/or thinking) in the numerator. The new combination could be:

$$\frac{S - R}{S} \quad \frac{\begin{array}{ll} \textbf{S} \text{ I value my career and} & \textbf{R} \text{ How can I order my time} \\ \text{family} & \text{so that I control my life} \\ & \textbf{both} \text{ at work and at home?} \end{array}}{\begin{array}{l} \textbf{S} \text{ I see many possibilities. I'm free to chose} \\ \text{what I think best. I can always change if my plan} \\ \text{is not working.} \end{array}}$$

In the new combination we have:

S - R	S vision	R order, control
S		S freedom, change

The effective helper understands that confusion is camouflaging the helpee's rational and supra-rational tendencies. The helper leads the helpee through the smoke-screen of confusion to get him in touch with his own rational and supra-rational tendencies. The following types of thinking are not necessarily irrational in themselves, but they tend to lead to irrational conclusions.

1. *Absolutizing*: "I'll *never* learn how to relate to him"; "I'll *never* understand that kid"; "He *always* tries to dominate people"; "I *always* fail."

   This type of absolutizing is irrational because it contradicts our rational and supra-rational tendencies. If, however, we say that we will *never* fly in this atmosphere by flapping our arms, we might be close to the truth.

2. *Either/or*: "You either love or hate me. I see that you hate me"; "I can't do two things at once; either I pay attention to myself or I pay attention to you."

   Some either/or statements make sense, but they usually refer to whether something exists and what that something is. For example , either God exists or does not exist. Suppose we say God exists, then God is good or bad, but not both. We can do the same kind of thinking about ourselves. We either exist or we don't exist. We are essentially good or bad as existing beings. It makes sense to say that we are all essentially good because to be, that is, to exist, is good. When we get into the question of *how* we are existing then we can say, "Sometimes I'm good, sometimes I'm bad." In describing *How* we are living we can use the concepts of *both* good *and* bad.

3. *Role/value thinking*: "I'm not a good parent, I'm not worth anything." "Obviously I'm valuable because I've been very successful." "If only I could get that promotion, I'd feel like I'm worth something."
   It's wise and socially useful to perform well in one's role. The moral and responsible thing to do is to work toward

performing well at whatever we think is valuable. However, our inherent worth as human beings does not depend on our performance.

4. *External cause/internal effect thinking:* "He makes me angry"; "The weather depresses me"; "He makes me feel like nothing"; "Look at what my parents have done to me."

This type of thinking clouds our supra-rational tendency of freedom. We are always free to choose the attitude that we will take toward people and events.

So how do we help someone think rationally? We don't have to give the helpee a course in logic. We can help him put order in his thinking by showing him how to get in touch with his supra-rational tendency of vision. The following are types of thinking that stimulate our intuition. Intuition is the mental activity at the center of vision. Have the helpee recall the positive past, that is, a moment in the past when he felt most like himself. Have him describe in detail that moment.

Conceptualizing: Have the helpee label his feelings, actions and thoughts of that positive moment with an all-embracing concept. For example, "It was a moment of freedom for me"; "It was a moment of unity for me"; "It was a moment of love for me."

Symbolizing: After the person has recalled and described a past positive experience in which he felt most like himself, ask him to imagine what the center of his being was like at that moment. Often people will symbolize their center with some form of light and/or movement, e.g., a rising golden light.

Translating: Translating means to change our vision into practice. Ask the helpee to imagine himself functioning in the area of his life where he has been experiencing confusion (his work, his relationships, his feelings about his future, etc.). Next, have him focus his attention on the symbol that represents what is important to him. Next, ask him to describe his feelings and behaviors as he sees himself functioning in his imagination in that area where he has been experiencing confusion. The helpee might say something like: I see myself feeling free with my wife. I see her disagreeing with me, but I'm not getting upset. I'm listening to her, but I'm also listening to myself. I'm concentrating on what is important to me *and* I'm trying to see what is important to her. I'm looking for some common ground to resolve our disagreement concerning how much time I'm putting into my career.

Translating our vision into the order of our life can be done effectively and quickly if we clearly see which operational concepts are consistent or are inconsistent with our ideal concepts. In the example above let's suppose that the helpee's ideal concepts (ICs) were love and freedom. As he imagines himself functioning according to his ideal concepts (ICs) he uses operational concepts (OCs) that are consistent with his ideal concepts, such as *listening* to his wife, *listening* to himself, *concentrating* on what is important to him, and *searching* for common ground.

When the helpee experiences confusion, he is probably using operational concepts (OCs), such as *arguing* to prove that he's right, *complaining* about his wife's behavior and *comparing* himself to other husbands that spend more time at their careers. Using OCs that are inconsistent with our IC's stirs up internal confusion. When we look at our operational concepts, that is, our thoughts about how we will act in the light of our ideal concepts, we can easily see which OCs are consistent with our ICs. For example we clearly see that forgiveness, an OC, is consistent with the IC of love and that revenge and holding back forgiveness are OCs inconsistent with love. However, even though we clearly see what we ought to do to order our life with love, we are free not to do so. At this point the helpee is ready to exercise the supra-rational tendency of freedom.

In dialoguing with the confused person that we want to help, our ultimate aim is to elicit responses from the spiritual dimension of the person. By that I mean we are using techniques, such as looking at assumptions, judging the reasonableness of expectations, labeling types of thinking, symbolizing values and translating values into new ways of thinking in order to evoke responses from the helpee's spiritual powers of self-reflection, intuition, ultimate choice and creativity. We don't have to be experts in the problem that plagues the person. We can be helpful to a parent having a difficult time without having a Ph.D. in family studies. If the parent is confused about being a parent, we can help him move from confusion to order to vision. At some point when specific knowledge is needed for a particular problem, such as alcoholism, a professional helper might be needed. But, generally speaking we can be helpful to people if we see the moves that they are making in life and if we know the moves they prefer to make. These moves can be represented by the IRS Human Tendencies Chart:

moving up

world-making
creativity
change
freedom
vision

order / control / system / certainty / self-profit

confusion   moving along
dependency
rebellion
skepticism
self-destruction

moving down

CHAPTER IX

Helping the Dependent Person

Before we describe the thoughts, behaviors and feelings of the dependent person and before we explain the strategies and techniques for helping the dependent person, let's once again look at the IRS Human Tendencies Chart. In the previous chapter I used steps going up and going down to show movement and the direction of our tendencies. Now I will put the tendencies side by side in rows to show their dynamic interrelationships.

Human Tendencies Profile

Irrational	Rational	Supra-Rational
confusion	order	vision
dependence	control	freedom
rebellion	system	change
skepticism	certainty	creativity
(move down toward)	(move toward)	(move up toward)
self-destruction	self-profit	making our world

We often experience the three types of tendencies simultaneously in the following groups.

Group I *Irrational*	*Rational*	*Supra-rational*
confusion	*order*	*vision*
(I just don't know what to do.)	(I have to get myself together.)	(I have to find out what is *really* important to me.)

Group II *Dependence* (I can't live without him.)	*Control* (I'm loosing it. I've got to take charge of my life.)	*Freedom* (I want a good relationship, but I want to feel free too.)
Group III *Rebellion* (I've taken too much from everyone at home, at work, everywhere. It's my turn to dish it out.)	*System* (This whole system of living is working against me. I need a new system.)	*Change* (It's time for me to change or to change things around me.)
Group IV *Skepticism* (What's the use of fighting it. There's no sure way to be happy.)	*Certainty* (I've got to feel sure about myself and the world around me.)	*Creativity* (I've got to come up with new ways of doing things.)
Self-destruction	*Self-profit*	*World Making*

We also experience these tendencies in a vertical progression. If we do not minimize our confusion by moving horizontally toward order and vision, then we move vertically downward toward self-destruction. A confused person can easily become dependent on drugs, someone else's mind, and on almost anything that provides an escape from confusion. Rebellion and skepticism usually follow dependence. For example, a person might have been confused about himself before entering a relationship. He might depend on the relationship to feel good about himself and to define himself. If the other person in the relationship withdraws, the dependent person will rebel against himself, the other person and all those in his life whom he *perceives* as a threat even though they are not a *real* threat to him. The next move he makes is toward skepticism and cynicism, "You can't trust anybody."

Suppose the person that we're helping is intensely experiencing skepticism. He feels depressed and alone. He sees no hope. He feels that he can not trust anyone. While experiencing skepticism, he is also slightly feeling the tendencies of certainty and creativity. The following diagram represents the relationship among the intensities of the three tendencies.

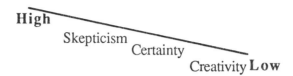

Helping here means to reverse the intensities to:

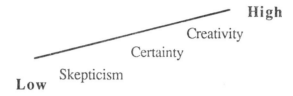

In order to help the person experiencing intense skepticism, we have to lead him through his rebellion, dependence and confusion to vision. The motivation to make the move back to initial confusion and over to vision will come from the spark of creativity buried under the debris of skepticism. The far away voice of creativity relentlessly calls out to him, "It's time to make a new life for yourself." If he were absolutely untouched by his supra-rational tendencies, he would not be seeking help. Furthermore, he would not even expect people to be trustworthy.

By mentally getting in touch first with the experience of rebellion, then the experience of dependence, and finally the experience of confusion, the skeptical person will understand how he moved to be where he is. Once he is in touch with his confusion, then he is prepared to move toward order and vision and onward to creativity.

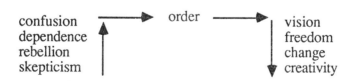

After getting in touch with his vision he can move vertically downward toward creativity and horizontally toward his rational tendencies. Helping, in terms of moving away from irrational tendencies, means moving up, moving across, moving down, moving between, moving back and forth.

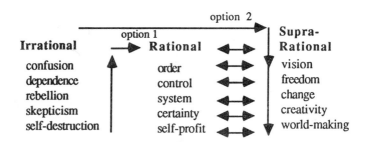

In this chapter we are concerned about helping the dependent person. We will describe the irrationally dependent person in relation to the rational tendency of control and the supra-rational tendency of freedom. Then we will examine some strategies and techniques for helping the dependent person move up, across and down to freedom.

How we surrender to the dominant tendency of irrational dependence

Although we come into this world as dependent children relying on others to satisfy our basic physical and psychological needs, the movement of human life aims at self-mastery and independence. Even as children we express our freedom and spontaneity. Early on in life we intuitively know that living ought to be expressive and not oppressive. Our intuitions are usually supported by our parents who freely and unconditionally express their love for us in infancy and early childhood. Yet, even those children whose parents neglect and abuse them still hold to their intuition telling them that to live is to give love freely.

No matter how the cards are stacked against us in our physical and psychological dimensions, we can always draw on our spiritual powers of intuition, self-reflection, ultimate choice and creativity to express ourselves positively. The following story taken from the *New York Times* of June 13, 1985 is an example of spiritual action.

DEAF, BLIND, AND NOW PH.D.

EUGENE, Ore. June 13, 1985 (AP)-- Shut off from the seeing and hearing world by blindness and deafness, Adeline Becht has proved herself in the classroom and is ready to take on the clinic.

The 48-year old Portland woman graduated today from the University of Oregon with two doctoral degrees in clinical and counseling psychology. She said she planned to expand her private counseling practice in Portland. In an interview with the *Oregon Journal*, Miss Becht said she lost her sight and hearing because of childhood drug addiction stemming from treatment for osteomyelitis and alcoholism. She said she can diagnose and treat psychological problems as effectively as her peers. My faith is very strong, she said.

Before moving on let's repeat that the development of our supra-rational tendencies requires the activity of our spiritual powers of intuition, self-reflection, ultimate choice and creativity. The activity of these powers requires the cooperation of our psychological and physical powers. For example, our power of intuition, by which we stay in touch with what and who is most important to us, is strong when our psychological processes of thinking, imagining and deciding and our physical power of moving our body here and there are in harmony with our intuition.

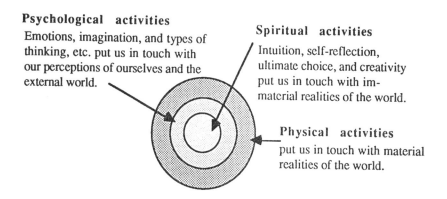

Psychological activities
Emotions, imagination, and types of thinking, etc. put us in touch with our perceptions of ourselves and the external world.

Spiritual activities
Intuition, self-reflection, ultimate choice, and creativity put us in touch with im-material realities of the world.

Physical activities
put us in touch with material realities of the world.

Who then is the irrationally dependent person and how does he get that way? Drug addicts, alcoholics and obsessive gamblers qualify as irrationally dependent people. These people seem to be the obvious examples of irrational dependency. However, most of us have experienced irrational dependency in not so obvious ways. Irrational dependency can even be a positive force. People that need to be needed in order to feel worthwhile disguise their irrational dependency with a veneer of altruism. Their concern for others is marred by their subtle attempt at possessiveness and control of other people. People that are always pushing themselves on other people to take care *of* instead of caring *for* them seem to exercise positive control on the surface. However, underneath they are excessively dependent on others needing them. Domineering parents fall into this category. Absolute authority and control shape their image of a parent more than reason and dialogue. In order to hold on to their image of being good parents, they depend on their children to be dependent on their parental control.

The following are some types of irrational dependencies:

1. *Seeking approval.*
   On the surface the person seeking approval appears docile, cooperative and generous. His intention, which can be clear but is often clouded, of gaining the approval of others corrupts his apparently virtuous behaviors. Even though he might be successful at eliciting praise from other people, deep down he does not feel like himself. He does not feel free. He feels continually anxious about losing the approval of others. He fears rejection more than anything else. He wants acceptance, but he feels trapped in the very acceptance that he feels he must have in order to feel good about himself.

2. *Trapped in an image.*
   An *image* that we have made for ourselves and that we *must* live up to is a *trap* that we have set for ourselves. When the ideals constituting our image, such as *perfection* as a parent or a professional, function as mental dictators compelling us to behave in certain ways, we do not feel free to change nor to think creatively. We are anxious about living up to our image, and we are depressed when we have failed to do so.

3. *Teachings/rewards dependency.*
   Growing up is a process of learning about life. The usual way of learning is to be taught. Parents, schools and churches pass on the wisdom of the ages to us in the form of doctrines. If we live by them, they work for us. "Work" means that we experience positive consequences for ourselves. The teachings of life tell us that the faithful practitioner of the teachings will be rewarded. Generally our own experiences confirm this line of thinking. However, we all discover sooner or later that behaving justly, lovingly, patiently and humbly is not always rewarded.

People that use teachings as they use programmed software in a computer are irrationally dependent. When they do not receive the outcome, the rewards, that were promised by the teachings, they become disillusioned, anxious, depressed, or somewhat alienated. When we allow teachings to become substitutes for our thinking instead of aids for our own self-reflection and creativity, then we become irrationally dependent.

We could list more types of dependencies, but I think the ones that we have described are the more general kinds functioning in the people that we are trying to help. Usually, people will not immediately identify their irrational dependency. They will recognize their feelings of being trapped, of being ill at ease with themselves, of having difficulty in developing an intimate relationship, of being fearful of truly expressing themselves, of worrying about directing their own lives and of being unsure about their own beliefs. Helping here means dialoguing to assist the person in labeling his emotions, behaviors and thinking. Then he will see the dominant tendency operating in his life.

The following lists of behaviors, emotions and types of thinking when combined make up irrational dependence:

Behaviors: seeking approval, looking for attention, seeking to please, always ready to follow, getting, holding, corralling people to ingratiate oneself, making unrealistic promises, demanding recognition.

Emotions: anxiety, depression, diffidence (lack of confidence), low self-esteem.

Thinking: scheming, image thinking, comparing, model thinking (trying to be like someone else), untested idealistic thinking, victim thinking (I did what I was supposed to do, I don't deserve this kind of treatment.)

Helping means to cooperate with the person to minimize the intensity of dependency and to maximize the intensity of freedom.

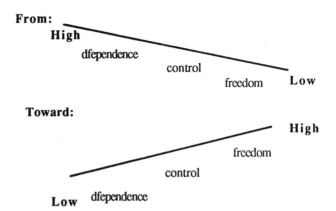

Strategy one: Move from dependence to confusion to order to vision to freedom

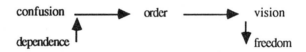

As we mentioned above, the person experiencing irrational dependence seeks help because he doesn't feel free. He wants to know *how* to feel free. But he needs to get in touch with where he is before he can move toward freedom. Dialoguing with him so that he labels his emotions, behaviors and types of thinking related to his particular concern (e.g., a relationship or work) is the first step. Step two is to let him identify his dominant tendency of dependence. As soon as he makes the connection among his behaviors, emotions and thinking, the label, irrational dependence, will flash before his mind's eye. Step three is to help him label his feelings and thoughts about himself. In this step he will recognize that he feels confused about himself. He will see that self-confusion led him into his irrational dependency. Step four is to move accross to the rational tendency of order by helping him get rid of his irrational assumptions and expectations about himself. Step five is to move toward vision by helping him get in touch with his activities of intuition and self-reflection. Steps three, four and five are the same steps that we used in helping the confused person. Step six is to help him get in touch with his tendency of freedom.

Let's make these steps more concrete by examining a person who is irrationally dependent on another person in a romantic relationship.

Helpee: I feel so bad about myself when I don't get the attention from him/her that I need. I expect much more than I'm getting. No matter what I do to get attention I fail.

Helper: (Identifies thinking, emotions and behaviors of helpee): You feel *depressed* about yourself when your *expectations* are not met and when *you fail to get attention.*

Helpee: Yes, I feel bad about myself. I know I shouldn't, but I do.

Helper: You feel confused about yourself when you are not treated the way you expect to be treated.

Helpee: Yes, I am confused.

Helper: Confused about...

Helpee: Confused about myself... Who am I? Am I worth anything to anybody?

Note: (At this point the helper can show the helpee the IRS Human Tendencies Profile. Ask the helpee if he/she can identify his/her operating tendencies and his/her wanted tendencies.)

Helper: (Moving toward order in helpee's thinking): Let's look at how you are thinking about yourself. You said that you feel confused about yourself when you are not treated the way you expect to be treated by him/her.

Helpee: Maybe I'm annoyed and angry, and then I'm confused... I'm not *really* an angry person.

Helper: So he/she doesn't make you angry and he/she doesn't confuse you about yourself, but you confuse yourself by letting yourself get angry. And you let yourself get angry because you demand that your expectations for affection be met. Do you really *need* attention to feel worthwhile?

Helpee: No...not really.

Helper. (Moving toward vision): Can you think of a time when you felt good about yourself, and you were not getting someone's attention?

Note: (At this point the helper is trying to suggest a
             way by which the helpee can get in touch with
             his/her powers of intuition and self-reflection.
             After the helpee recalls a positive experience,
             then the helper suggests that he/she stays in
             touch with the feelings, thoughts, images and
             behaviors of that positive experience, while at
             the same time, he/she visualizes the person
             refusing to give him/her attention. Then the
             helper asks the helpee how he/she *chooses* to
             respond to the other person. At this point the
             helpee ought to experience a tendency of
             freedom.)

**Strategy Two: Moving between vision and order and
between freedom and control**

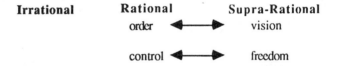

When irrational dependence dominates someone's life, he feels
controlled. Helping someone move from dependence to freedom
means assisting someone to take control of his life. The dialogue in
strategy two might go something like the following:

Helper: (Reflecting the helpee's internal feeling of self-
             worth): So when you are in touch with yourself,
             you experience a sense of abiding internal
             worth. And the circumstances that help you get
             in touch with your own value are when you are
             in touch with nature and when you listen to
             music.
Helpee:.   Yes. Then I feel that I have true respect for my-
             self.
Helper: How does that feeling of self-worth and self-re-
             spect affect your relationships?

Helpee: Well...I treat others as I would treat myself.
            (The helper is trying to help the helpee identify a
            principle that will order his thinking.)
Helper: If you use that idea of respecting others as you
            respect yourself to direct your behaviors in your
            relationship with _____, what
            different responses can you think of when you
            do not get attention?
Note: (The helper is assisting the helpee to think in
            possibilities so that he/she sees that he/she has
            choices. He/she can control his/her emotions,
            behaviors and thinking in relationships. The
            helpee also realizes the possible consequences of
            his/her choice. By exercising his/her vision and
            freedom the relationship might end or it might
            change to a healthy one.)

Strategy three: Moving between freedom and control and down from order to control

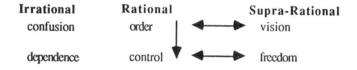

As long as the helpee stays in touch with his vision of himself by doing the mental and physical exercises that facilitate his intuition of himself, such as meditation, self-dialogue about what and who are ultimately important to him, using his memory to recall those prized moments when he felt most like himself, using his constructive imagination to see himself moving on in life courageously and assuredly, and using his reason to foresee many ways to live out his vision of himself, he will feel free. He will feel free *from irrationally depending* on the approval of someone for a feeling of self-worth, and he will feel free *to choose* ways of responding to people and events.

Suppose you are trying to help a teenager that feels moody and depressed. Suppose that the teenager feels that his peers and/or parents think little of him. He feels that he is faceless and insignificant, because he believes that others believe that he is a "nerd." His low feelings about himself make him move like a "nerd." Because he behaves according to what he believes that others believe about him, his peers avoid him and his parents are always asking him, "what's wrong with you?" He feels depressed and anxious because deep down he is *not* accepting that he *is* worthless. He *feels* worthless, but he intuitively knows that he *is* worthwhile. Since he is psychologically confused, he is ready to fall into the dependency trap of looking for approval. Suppose we help him sort out his irrational thinking accounting for the major part of his confusion, and suppose he is now in touch with his true vision of himself. Now we are ready to help him move from vision to order and from freedom to control.

Helper	(reflecting helpee's feelings of freedom and self-worth): You are speaking with more determination, moving around with more bounce and you seem to have a clear sense of yourself. You move like a person that cares for himself and is ready to care for others.
Helpee:	Yeah...I'm feeling good about myself, but I'm worried about losing that feeling. When people put me down, it's tough to bounce back.
Helper	(Constructing with the helpee an order of beliefs about relating to people that flows from the helpee's vision of himself): How do you think you ought to respond to people that give you a hard time?
Helpee:	Give them some of their own medicine...but that's not me.
Helper:	So you want to be yourself in responding to them. Stay in touch with your feelings about yourself and visualize yourself responding to a put-down.
Helpee:	I don't feel threatened. I hear myself saying to myself, "So what? His opinion doesn't change me."
Helper:	So you feel confident about yourself, but you don't want to play his game?
Helpee:	My game is to respect myself and respect others.
Note:	(At this point the helpee has identified the principle that orders his thinking. The next move is to translate that principle into action so that he takes *control* of himself and of the interaction between himself and his peers.)

Helper	(Helping the helpee to think in possibilities): So you have a lot of ways to respond to this guy who just put you down.
Helpee	(Exploring): Yeah...I could walk away; I could ask him what's bugging him; I could tell him that he can have his opinion; I could tell him that he has a habit of dumping on other people. Yeah...I can chose to do a lot of things.

In this strategy we were working with the helpee to translate his vision into practice by constructing an order of beliefs that was consistent with his vision. Then, we moved between freedom and control so that the helpee felt free to choose a course of action among many options. The final move would be from order to control when the helpee decides on a particular response.

We ought to keep in mind that true helping means assisting someone in developing true freedom. This principle is extremely important for people in authority, especially parents. When this principle is violated, the once-upon-a-time docile child becomes rebellious. In the next chapter we will present some strategies for helping the rebellious person.

Chapter X

Helping the Rebellious Person

The grandiosely rebellious person flaunts his anger. He usually despises most of the people in the world and disdainfully ignores "the system" and social civilities. The worst case of the rebellious person is the violent criminal inflicting physical pain with pleasure. The more common case of the outwardly rebellious type is the alienated person discharging psychological venom on his family, neighbors and business associates. We usually refer to this type as crude, nasty and mean. A few degrees lower on the scale of rebellion, we find the moaners, the groaners and the complainers These people find something wrong with almost everything and everyone except themselves.

The *quietly* rebellious person conceals his anger under the cloak of conformity or behind the mask of cynical humor. The angry conformer externally accepts "the system" but internally rejects it. The system could be any aspect of his culture, such as the school system, organized religion or the corporation's way of doing business. Outwardly he cannot reject the system because he depends on it for the satisfaction of his physical and psychological needs. Since he restrains his anger, he suffers from implosion. He feels pressures pushing *in* on him. From time to time he lets off steam aimlessly to undo the knot in his stomach. His behavior is inexplicable to others. In time his outbursts multiply, then other people label him "a nervous person," who has to be approached carefully. Instead of letting his anger emerge volcanically, the quietly rebellious person sometimes chooses the defense of submerging his anger deeper by behaving just the opposite. He will "lovingly" condescend to others rather than attack them. The pressure to conform subdues his aggressive impulses. Underneath, he feels resentful.

In helping the rebellious person we are working with the following set of tendencies:

Irrational	*Rational*	*Supra-Rational*
rebellion	system	change

The rebellious person usually seeks help in order to change someone else or the system. Whether the person is outwardly rebellious or inwardly rebellious, his own rebellion wears him down. Rebellion does not bring about productive change. So, he becomes tired and frustrated. He needs some help, someone to show him what to do. Helping the rebellious person means to cooperate with him to identify the real source of his oppression.

The following are some of the behaviors, ways of thinking and emotions experienced by the rebellious person:

Behaviors: complaining, whining, compulsive fault-finding, hitting things, throwing things, uses violent language, sometimes joins revolutionary groups, fakes cooperation and then foot-drags, envious of others, worries a lot.

Ways of thinking: very rigid concepts about how the world should be; either/or thinking; has difficulty thinking in grey areas; thinks empirically, that is, only sense knowledge is true knowledge; thinks mechanically, that is, puts ideas together the way he puts parts of a machine together; thinks ego-centrically, that is, something is worthwhile only if it is self-satisfying.

Emotions: anger, frustration, anxiety, apprehension.

The behaviors and emotions of grandiose rebellion are strikingly stronger than those of quiet rebellion. However, the ways of thinking in both types of rebellion could be similar. An extroverted person would tend to be outwardly rebellious, whereas an introverted person would tend to be inwardly rebellious. The extrovert is more conscious of the external world of things and people. His responses to the world, whether positive or negative, are direct and visible. The introvert is more conscious of the internal world of ideas and images. His responses to the world, whether positive or negative, are reserved and cryptic. Both the introvert and extrovert, nevertheless, might have very rigid concepts about how the world and people should be. They present people with an either/or proposition: either think my way and be with me, *or* think your way and be against me. The extrovert would be very open and direct in expressing his anger toward those that don't accept his ideas. The introvert would express his anger indirectly by ignoring or dismissing as ignorant those that don't accept his ideas.

Our major objective in helping the rebellious person is to minimize the irrational tendency of rebellion and to maximize the supra-rational tendency of change.

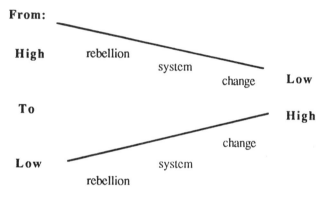

Strategy one: Moving up from rebellion to dependence to confusion.

Irrational	Rational	Supra-Rational
confusion	order	vision
dependence	control	freedom
rebellion	system	change

As we said above, the rebellious person seeks help because he feels worn out and tired. His presenting problem is, "What am I going to do with these people that are getting in my way?" *These people* could be parents, bosses, spouses, children, business associates, colleagues, government officials, clerks, taxi drivers and almost anybody on any given day. But, usually, the rebellious person complains about people close to him.

Let's take the case of a young adult that feels rebellious primarily toward his parents. In the course of our conversation with him we discover that he is suffering from a creeping rebellion. He is striking out at his business associates and girlfriend. Let's suppose that he is a mixture of inward rebellion toward his parents and outward rebellion toward everyone else. In dialoguing with him we want to help him get in touch with the real source of his anger so that he will focus his attention on changing himself rather than trying to change everyone else.

Helper:	(Reflecting helpee's anger after helpee complained about the people at work): You feel very angry toward the people at work. Is there someone in particular toward whom you feel great anger?
Helpee:	Yeah...my boss, but I can't blast off at him. He's a real ass.
Helper:	(Connecting anger to behavior): When you're angry at your boss how do you show it?
Helpee:	I usually ignore him. I guess I take it out on the people around me too.
Helper:	(Connecting thinking to helpee's anger and behaviors): I guess you're saying something to yourself about your boss when you're angry.
Helpee:	Yeah...I'm saying that he is an incompetent and manipulative bastard. He tries to control everyone...doesn't respect anyone's ideas. I could do a much better job than him.
Helper:	(Sorting out helpee's self-talk to identify helpee's assumptions, expectations, type of thinking and values): You value your own ideas and you expect your boss to value them also. I wonder if you're assuming that he should think the way you think.
Helpee:	Hell no! He can think the way he wants as long as he and all his "yes" people stay out of my way.
Helper:	(Connecting type of thinking to helpee's anger and passive aggression toward his boss): You seem to be saying to your boss, "Either respect my ideas *or* I'll screw you every chance I get."
Helpee:	Yeah. That's about it. He makes me so angry.

Helper: (Confronting helpee on who is responsible for his anger): if your boss *makes* you angry, he seems to have great power over you. He seems to be your oppressor.

Helpee: Well...When I say, "He makes me angry," he doesn't...you know *make me* angry. I get angry because he's in my way.

Helper: (Reflecting helpee's ownership of his anger): So *you* get angry, that is *you* make yourself angry.

Helpee: Yeah...I guess so.

Helper: (Exploring to find helpee's defense preventing him from looking at himself): If you make yourself angry, what do you get out of it?

Helpee: Well, it feels good.

Helper: (Helper files this response in the back of his mind. He will explore the roots of the helpee's anger in strategy two.) For a while, but afterwards you feel worn and frustrated.

Helpee: Right. He's still in my way.

Helper: (Identifying helpee's confusion and dependence): It seems that you are tying to do something worthwhile at work. You believe that you have good ideas, and you want to get them into operation. On the other hand you seem to expect your boss to accept your ideas unconditionally. You seem to be angry at him for not approving you.

Helpee: Maybe that makes sense. Maybe I'm angry at myself for not having enough confidence and courage to keep trying when things get tough.

Up to this point the helper has been working with the helpee to move from rebellion by showing the helpee that rebellion is the consequence of dependence and confusion. His real oppressors are his own irrational dependence and confusion. He feels dependent because he is confused about his own powers and his relationship to his boss.

Strategy Two: Moving across to order and to vision.

We have already explained this strategy in the two previous chapters. The basic idea is to sort out the emotions, behaviors and thinking making up the helpee's irrational tendency of confusion in order to clearly identify the sources of his confusion. In our example above we said that the young adult was primarily rebellious toward his parents, however, in the dialogue I had him talk only about his anger toward his boss and his business associates. Now, in strategy two we want to explore the helpee's other relationships to see if a pattern of anger pervades his life.

Helper: (Exploring with the helpee to map out the extent of his anger): You are openly angry with your peers, but inwardly angry with your boss. I wonder if you experienced that combination of anger at any other time in your life.

Helpee: Many times I was angry with my parents, but I never expressed it openly. I let it out on other people, I guess.

Helper: (Helping him to get in touch with his self-talk): What were you saying to yourself, when you were angry with your parents?

Helpee: "I can never please them. They're always criticizing me. Some day I'll show them. I'll show everybody," that's what I'd tell myself.

Helper: So, you were out to prove yourself to your parents.

Helpee: Yeah... but I never succeeded.

Helper: (Connecting thinking, emotions and behaviors that combined to make up his confusion): So you assumed that when you would meet your parents' expectations, you would feel good about yourself, but the more you tried, the more frustrated you became, and then, you felt worse about yourself and more angry with them. You probably felt confused at first, and then you depended on them for approval. When you didn't get their approval you became rebellious.

Helpee: Yeah... that's about it. (He realizes that his poor thinking affected the order of his life.)

Helper: (Connecting rebellion toward parents with rebellion toward boss): Maybe the same story is taking place with you and your boss.

Helpee: I think so.

Helper: (Moving to vision): Let's leave your parents and boss aside and let's find out what's most important to you in your work.

Strategy Three: Moving down from vision through freedom to change and across to system.

So far the movement has been up an across.

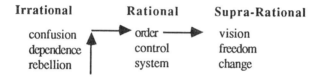

To help the helpee move from vision to change we will repeat the same strategies that we used in the two previous chapters, namely, moving down from vision to freedom, between vision and order, between freedom and control.

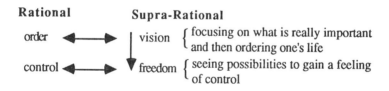

Having completed the moves between vision and order, between freedom and control, and down from order to control, we are ready to use this strategy in which the helpee chooses a course of action that will produce a positive change. In our example of the angry young adult let's assume that cooperation, results and implementing his own ideas make up part of his vision of himself at work. The next step is to freely develop his options that will change his ideals into operational concepts. He might choose dialoguing with others as a concept that will actualize his ideal of cooperation and of implementing his ideas. The next step is to make the necessary changes, particularly in himself, to make the concept of dialogue work. Those changes might mean learning more about the art of communicating and about monitoring his self-talk and behaviors, so that he does not slip back into rebellion. In this strategy the helpee becomes more aware of changes as an on-going process, rather than a one-shot deal. This strategy will propose ways of thinking and behaving that are just the opposite of those that make up rebellion.

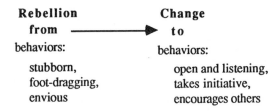

Rebellion
from ⟶ **Change**
to

behaviors: behaviors:

stubborn,   open and listening,
foot-dragging,   takes initiative,
envious   encourages others

Our objective in this strategy is to help him explore the consequences that his change of thinking and behaving will have on his system of living. In other words, how will a change in one area of his life affect the other areas of his life.

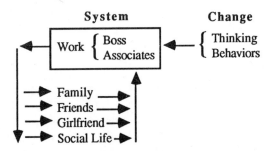

System   **Change**

Work { Boss   { Thinking
       Associates   Behaviors

Family
Friends
Girlfriend
Social Life

In changing his ways of thinking and of behaving at work the helpee might experience tensions in other areas of his life requiring change. By moving between change and system the helpee will develop an awareness of himself and life as a process, that is, from a challenge we move to a solution, and then the solution becomes another challenge. For example, getting a college degree at one point in our life is a solution. When we graduate, the college degree presents us with a challenge, "What will I do with it?" The technique that we will use in this strategy is *exploring the possible consequences in other areas of his life* that the helpee's contemplated change, dialoguing, could produce.

Helper: So you have chosen to develop the skill of dia-
            loguing with your boss and colleagues in order
            to get your ideas into practice and to be true to
            your vision of life.
Helpee: Yeah...what I really want is to bring about pro-
            ductive change. All this rebellion on my part just
            leads to destruction. I'll really have to work at
            developing that skill of dialoguing.
Helper: What will you be required to do?
Helpee: I'll have to learn it. I'll have to block out some
            time to do some reading, maybe go back to
            school.
Helper: How will the reorganization affect the other
            areas of your life?
Helpee: I guess I'll be putting more pressure on myself
            to do something about the way I've got to
            concentrate on what is important to me and to
            keep in mind that my self-worth doesn't depend
            on their approval. I've got to be patient with
            myself also.
Helper: (Getting helpee ready for the next move toward
            creativity): It seems that you will have to do
            some creative thinking to renew yourself.

Rebellion as a Neurotic disorder and Rebellion as a Character Disorder

A person suffers neurotic disorder when he *feels* that he can't manage the pressures and frustrations that are normally encountered in the processes of living. The neurotic prefers static stability. But living is a series of changes. The person suffering from neurotic rebellion wants a change to end all change. When change is eliminated he will have a static system of life without the tensions and ambiguities of change. His idea of peace is equated with external comfort and convenience. Everyone and everything, his parents, his spouse, his children, his colleagues and his work will finally be in place once and for all according to his blueprint. When the system is perfect, that is, set and purged of all disturbances he will be happy. We all have a longing for that kind of tranquility, that kind of rest. Our dream world usually pops into mind when we *feel* anxious about facing up to the tensions of living. In those moments we all feel a touch of neuroticism. The difference between the anxious person functioning well and the anxious person not functioning well is that the well-functioning person separates what he *feels* from what he *believes* that he can do. The well-functioning person takes charge of his thinking to make sure that he does not think distortedly of himself. A person succumbing to his anxiety tries to dominate the people and the world out there. His neuroticism takes the form of irrational rebellion.

Incipient teenage rebellion is special and normal. Teenagers feel the pull between dependency and autonomy. Their feeling of autonomy emerges with the development of their mental ability to think for themselves. When they were younger they rebelled against their parents because what their parents wanted was *uncomfortable* for them. As teenagers they rebel because what their parents want seems *unreasonable* to them. In helping teenagers we have to keep in mind that their incipient rebellion over different issues, such as staying out at night, using the car, money matters, dating, etc, is not neurotic. They are discovering their own strengths. Helping teenagers means cooperating with them in such a way that they get in touch with their own intuition about what and who is important to them. They have to learn how to give themselves orders that make sense to themselves. Ordering teenagers around autocratically, that is, without reasoning with them, could influence them to doubt the quality of their own thinking. If they feel doubtful about their powers to think and to decide, they are ripe for irrational confusion and rebellion. Adults can be a forceful factor in precipitating incipient teenage rebellion into neurotic teenage rebellion.

To understand rebellion as a *character* disorder we have to see how the person is using the spiritual power of ultimate choice. The power of ultimate choice is the activity of deciding on our central value and our ultimate reality. By ultimate reality we mean who or what is the center of the universe. Some people choose to place themselves at the center of the universe while others choose to recognize a reality beyond them as the ultimate reality, such as, God, Nature, Humankind, etc. If a person chooses himself to be the center of the universe he usually rejects the world in the way he finds it. He says "No" to it. The world has to be the way he says it must be. However, proclaiming a change does not make a change. So, grabbing power becomes the central value of the person who sees himself as the center of the universe and who autocratically tries to twist the world into shapes that match his own ideas of it.

When a person chooses to say "No" to the world, to say "No" to cooperating with others and to say "No" to his own limitations, he has chosen the character, that is, the distinctive mark of rebellion. He is the person that gives ulcers and does not get ulcers. The rebellious character is usually the getting, dominating and manipulating type. Unlike the rebellious neurotic that functions poorly, the rebellious character functions fairly well, that is, anxiety does not disrupt his daily activities. The rebellious character does not show signs of neurotic anxiety; however, he behaves in socially useless ways. People experiencing a dominant tendency of rebellion feel angry and hostile but they also feel guilt and remorse. These people do not have a rebellious character. They sincerely choose to say "Yes" to life, but they do not know how, or they are too afraid to live out that "Yes." For example, they want to trust in the ultimate goodness in themselves and in life, but they have failed too often or have been hurt by others too often to live out that trust. They are experiencing disorder in their personality, that is, disruption among their emotions, behaviors and thinking preventing them from making their world according to their best intuitions. The following diagram shows the relationship among character, personality and temperament.

Temperament
Our particular biological organization through which and with which we express our character and personality.

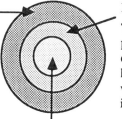

Personality
The particular organization of our psychological systems, such as emotions, thinking and behaviors that help or hinder us in making our world according to our best intuitions.

Character Determined by the particular use or disuse of our spiritual activities of intuition, self-reflection, ultimate choice and creativity.

The adage, "you can't tell a book by its cover," applies to helping people. By temperament some people look depressed, and some look vivacious. A little exploring into both types could reveal just the opposite. The apparently happy person feels depressed, and the apparently depressed person is peaceful. To be truly helpful we have to listen to the character of the person. Once the person reveals his character, then we can cooperate with him in dialogue to discover the ways by which he will make his world.

Chapter XI

HELPING THE SKEPTICAL PERSON

Skeptical people lack a basic sense of trust in themselves and in others. They rarely seek help directly. They believe that people really don't care about them. However, before taking the decisive step toward self-destruction, they will send out vague messages for help. They will disguise their need for help just enough, so that only perceptive and sensitive people will recognize their appeal for assistance. How often have our good intentions and good will to help been tested by someone saying something like, "It's a tough world out there. People don't have time to listen to one another. When you feel that your career is going down the tubes, who cares?" The central issue for the skeptical person is trust. Many negative events and unresponsive people have contributed to the lack of trust in skeptical persons. Self-centered parents neglecting their children in infancy and early childhood tell their children by their actions that people are unreliable. Teenagers lose trust in others when their "friends" turn out to be disloyal and when authority figures treat their ideas and feelings lightly. Institutions, such as governments and churches that seem to behave inconsistently, are often perceived by teenagers and young adults as not trustworthy. Although negative events and unreliable people contribute to their doubts about the trustworthiness of people, they still have the power to hope in the ultimate goodness of people.

When helping the skeptical person, we have to keep in mind that we are cooperating with him to move from skepticism to creativity.

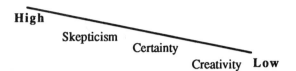

Helping here means to reverse the intensities to:

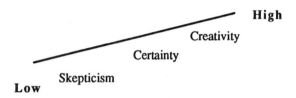

A covert desire for certainty underlies the overt skepticism of the person lacking trust. When a person moves continually between skepticism and certainty he forms a mental whirlpool dragging him down to self-destruction. For example, suppose we do not trust someone with whom we must work. We want to be one-hundred percent certain that he will not deceive us. But, we cannot get one-hundred percent certainty *before* we interact with him. Our distrust will lead us to examine all the possible ways he can deceive us. Then, we will have to look for ways to protect ourselves. We want to be absolutely certain that we will not be cheated. But our experience tells us that we cannot be absolutely certain about anybody. To protect ourselves we withdraw. In isolating ourselves from others we eventually destroy ourselves. This same kind of whirlpool develops when we try to protect ourselves from making mistakes. Because we do not trust our own intuition and good judgment, we look for absolute and certain answers before we make a decision on any important matter. But, our own skepticism prevents us from accepting any answers as certain. Consequently, we put off making decisions.

To help a skeptical person means to develop his awareness of novelty, surprise and risk hidden in his tendency of creativity. As soon as the person suffering from neurotic skepticism sees that his skepticism is choking his life instead of expanding it, he will be ready to do what is necessary to move toward creativity. He will see that by responding to the tendency of creativity he will genuinely enlarge and enrich his life. He will be willing to face what prevents him from trusting and risking. He will be ready to see what he is required to do to remove the obstacles on his way to creativity.

How the skeptic avoids his feelings about himself

The skeptical person having been hurt by the neglect and coldness of people in the past insulates himself from the warm emotions of other people and douses the sparks of any affectionate feelings that he feels toward others. He does not want to reach out toward others nor reach in toward himself. He has a repertoire of defenses:

1. Explaining away positive feelings of others

Fearful of becoming trapped in someone else's positive emotion, the skeptic will defuse the personal quality of an emotion by giving a perfectly rational and objective explanation for such an outburst of human energy. If someone shows him affection, he will explain it away by saying something like: "Her genes make her very expressive in her responses, but they also make her inconsistent."

2. Morbid Introspection

Not trusting his own positive emotions, the skeptic is his own muckraker. He looks for the evil intention behind his "good feelings" toward others and toward himself. The belief in love for oneself and another is not a deep-rooted conviction in his character. Instead of trusting the simplicity and honesty of his feelings of love, he believes that these feelings are crooked expressions of his own self-deception. Since he believes that he *cannot* love, he must probe his psyche until he finds the real evil motivation behind the mask of love. In examining his feelings of altruism, he might say to himself, "What *I* am really concerned about in this relationship is, 'What's in it for me?'"

3. Mining the home port

The skeptic prevents intimate contact by setting up obstructions such as, a strict schedule that makes him scarce for human contact; an announced list of do's and don'ts that is intended to put off people; a subtle but rigid review program that people must pass before he shows any signs of trust toward them; a vague vocabulary stacked with words like perhaps, eventually, potentially, maybe, etc., that helps him dodge any commitment; and, a rule of consulting no one and of counseling no one. All these defenses act as mines preventing hostile ships from slipping into the home port.

What prevents a person lacking trust in himself and in others from taking the decisive step toward self-destruction? How can a person live a lonely, self-centered and suspicious life of skepticism for a long time? The tendency of skepticism works in conjunction with the rational tendency of certainty and minimally with the supra-rational tendency of creativity.

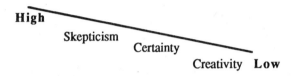

The moving force behind skepticism is the rational desire to be certain. However, it is irrational to expect absolute rational certainty in human relationships. Reason tells us that people are free to love or not to love, to trust or not to trust, to forgive or not forgive, and even to grow or not to grow. But rational certainty for the skeptic means protection against the inconsistent behavior of humans. However, unless we are in touch with our supra-rational tendencies of vision and freedom, our rational desire for certainty will be guided by our irrational tendency of skepticism. We will be more aware of the negative side of life. Certainty will mean securing ourselves against the aggressiveness of other people. The skeptic wants to be absolutely certain about his own security. The strength of his rational tendency of certainty prevents him from throwing up his hands in despair. In a sense the skeptic is an embattled person fighting for his psychological survival.

Strategy one: Moving from skepticism toward certainty and creativity

To help the skeptic means to help him move from viewing to doing. The person lacking in trust does not get involved with anyone or in anything that he can't control. The skeptic is very cautious. He weighs the pros and cons. He looks at all the angles. We have to use a technique that will move him from critical looking and talking to constructive doing.

Sculpting clay is a technique that can help him get in touch with different aspects of his skepticism as well as with his concealed tendency of creativity. A lump of clay in the hands of a skeptic will be exactly that...a lump of clay. He will balance it to check its weight. He will poke at it to check its consistency. He will revolve it with his finger to gauge its dimensions. He will not commit himself to do anything with it until he feels a sense of subjective certainty, that is, a sense of control to make it into something predictable, such as a cube, a sphere, or a cylinder. If we suggest that he do something different with the clay, we will be helping him to get in touch with his feelings of novelty and spontaneity. He will let go of his desire for certainty and control. The malleability of the clay will suggest novel forms to him. If he lets his fingers follow his intuition and the possibilities latent in the clay, he will experience fun, novelty and surprise.

The next step is to help him reflect on his thoughts and feelings as he was sculpting the clay. At this point it is important for him to express his feelings of trust in his own creativity. It is also important for him to realize that genuine feelings of security grow out of trust.

The final step in this strategy is to help him see the analogy between sculpting clay and sculpting his world of human relationships. He will be quick to see the glaring differences between sculpting inert clay and relating to sometimes volatile and always mysterious human beings. The outcome of a human relationship, he will point out, is not determined by one person alone. We will agree with him that the quality and form of a human relationship is the product not only of creativity, but also of cooperation. The skeptic will be willing to change provided he can trust in himself. The next move will be to help him get in touch with his vision.

Strategy Two: Moving up from skepticism to confusion and across to vision

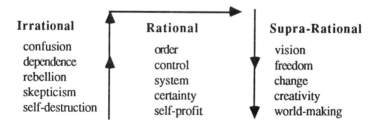

Irrational	Rational	Supra-Rational
confusion	order	vision
dependence	control	freedom
rebellion	system	change
skepticism	certainty	creativity
self-destruction	self-profit	world-making

As I said above the skeptic is an embattled person. He is warding off destruction from without and from within.

From within

1. He doubts his own ultimate goodness. He believes that there are more evil forces than good forces within him.

2. He is afraid to express himself genuinely and honestly to another person out of fear of being rejected. Because he doubts his own goodness, he believes that other people will put on a false face.

3. He doubts his own intellectual, social, physical and artistic abilities. To protect himself against his underestimation of himself he will strive to achieve in those areas of life where success can be tangibly measured. Having money, power and prestige is important to the skeptic. These types of external security make up for his lack of internal security.

From without

1. The negative influences of the immediate family contribute greatly to the skeptic's suspicious attitude. His tendency to be close to someone with whom he could share his deepest thoughts and feelings was not nurtured by his mother or father. Sometimes this gap is filled by a trusted friend or an older person that substitutes as a big brother or sister. In the case of the skeptic the gap was never filled, or a trusted relationship was not sustained over a long period of time. The skeptic loses trust because someone is not *always* there for him. His family is not a source of hope for him. He either drifts away from his parents and his brothers and sisters, or he reacts to them out of duty.

2. When the skeptic marries, he hopes against his own lack of hope. Marriage will be his salvation. The course of his life will finally be set straight. All the affection, attention and intimacy that his family denied him will be given to him in marriage. If his expectations are not met by his marriage partner to his satisfaction, he will be singing his old theme song, "You can't trust anybody."

3. Success at work is important to the skeptic. Although he feels that advancement in his career is within his control, he knows that he will not get ahead without being vigilant. Moving up the ladder of success is like playing a game for the skeptic. Your opponent is out there to make you lose. The skeptic sees his co-workers as opponents in the game of life. They are necessary for the game. But they cannot be trusted. They are out there to get his job.

To help the skeptic move from skepticism to vision means to help develop a sense of internal power based on a true vision of himself. Before moving ahead let's review the three dimensions of a person and some of the activities of each dimension.

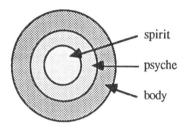

If one of our irrational tendencies is stronger than our rational and supra-rational tendencies, then we feel as if we are falling apart. The irrational tendencies are dominant because all the activities of the spirit are not operating harmoniously. In the case of the skeptic, self-reflection is operating overtime, whereas the other three activities of intuition, ultimate choice (will) and creativity are shut-down. The psychological activities of remembering and self-talk are focusing on the content of the skeptic's self-reflection. The skeptic's reflection about himself is mostly negative because of the negative influences in his life and/or because of his own failures. Consequently, his self-talk is, "You can't trust anybody," and his memory recalls all his negative experiences to support the "fact" of the untrustworthiness of people. His body activities are very much influenced by the activities of his spirit and psyche. His desire for sex might be repressed, and he might develop several habits that reflect his lack of trust, such as checking on the actions of other people as well as his own. He will hardly ever take the word of another that the lights are out, the back door is locked and the burglar alarm is set before leaving the house. He will have to see for himself. As we have seen, the chain of interactions among the spirit, psyche and body depend in the final analysis on the interactions among the activities of the spirit.

In the case of the skeptic intuition, ultimate choice and creativity are not operating to enrich self-reflection. The skeptic is hyper-reflective about the negative experiences of life because his intuition of his own inherent goodness is not active. His intuition is not active because his power of ultimate choice, that is, his will to see his own goodness, is suspended. Consequently, he is not enriching his life through his power of creativity by which he can symbolize to himself the new world that he can make.

Helping the skeptic move to vision means:

1. To lead him to confront his own rebellion toward other people, such as his parents and friends who were in fact not trustworthy, or that he *believed* were not trustworthy. To confront a past negative experience means to recall as accurately as possible the events, the emotions and the thoughts of that experience. As he stands before the images of these negative experiences, we can confront him with a choice by saying, "You can choose to be a victim of those negative experiences. You can close yourself off like a clam from the rest of the world. *Or* you can choose to get in touch with the positive experiences of yourself." By using the technique of self-confrontation, we are helping the skeptic get in touch with the spiritual activities of ultimate choice (either/or decision) and intuition (recalling positive experiences of himself). Then, we can help him confront his psychological activities of irrational thinking, such as generalizing about the untrustworthiness of *all* people based on his own negative experiences of *some* people. As he straightens out his thinking, he will become more aware of his distorting habits, such as stinginess and checking on everyone and everything.

Helping the skeptic move to vision means:

2. To get him in touch with his irrational dependency. We can all use the affection and attention of our parents when we are young and even throughout our adult years. However, the skeptic never symbolically cut the psychological umbilical cord linking his feelings about himself with his parents' attention toward him. He let his image of himself and his feelings of self-worth depend very much on the flow of attention coming from his parents. When that attention was dried up or just trickled down occasionally, the skeptic would force the attention of his parents on him by doing something disruptive. Then, he was told that he was bad. Psychologically, he was trapped. He couldn't trust himself, because he believed that he was bad, and he couldn't trust his parents because he knew that they would not affirm his goodness.

We can use the technique of immediacy to help the skeptic confront his irrational dependency. Immediacy means to help the skeptic label the feelings that he is now experiencing toward the helper. Immediacy, that is, being in touch with and expressing the feelings that the helper and helpee are experiencing toward each other right then and there, will keep both on the alert for latent but creeping feelings of dependency. The worst scenario that could develop between the helper and the skeptic is a relationship of irrational dependency in which the helper is the savior and the skeptic is the saved. The aim here is to help the skeptic get in touch with his intuition and self-reflection, so that he will feel psychologically free in his discussions with the helper. He will feel free to do self-exploration and self-reflection to discover and symbolize his own inherent value. We will truly have helped the skeptic when he discards his skepticism, because he experiences the realities of trust, equality and independence with us.

The symptoms of skepticism

1. *Using drugs*

Underlying the tendency of skepticism is the type of thinking that says, "The only things that are real are the things you can see, touch, smell, hear and taste." Pleasant sensations are the only worthwhile and trustworthy experiences. We feel good about ourselves, so the belief goes, when we are having pleasant sensations. *If* we accept the questionable belief that happiness means ultimately having pleasant sensations, then whether or not we use drugs is not the problem for us. *The* problem for people whose only measure of truth is sensation, is *how* to use them, so that they stay physically sound and physically pleased continuously.

Too often we are disturbed by "the drug problem" for the wrong reasons. We are upset over the destructive consequences of the uncontrolled use of drugs. We look at "the drug problem" as a behavioral problem. "The drug problem," however, is really a symptom of a "thinking problem." If we have no thinking powers to put us in touch with realities beyond sensation, then we can only trust our sensations. It's not surprising that many materially successful people have a "drug problem." A little probing will reveal that they believe in nothing beyond what their senses tell them. Some, however, hope that their sensations empowered by drugs will touch the unseen realities in which they do not believe. They will believe in the unseen realities only when they see them. For them seeing is believing. Until then, all that is real is what can be sensed. Therefore, love means only sex. Justice means owning what you paid for. Truth means what you can see and touch. Self-worth means having good sensations about yourself. "So...why not try drugs to have it all? If we feel good, take drugs to feel better. If we feel bad, take drugs to feel good." However, that type of thinking, as the evidence shows, leads to self-destruction, the final step after skepticism.

2. *The mania for having*

Many people make up for their lack of belief in themselves and others by having possessions. Their feelings of security are the fruits of their fat bank accounts, their big cars, their fully equipped houses, their luxury boats and whatever else they call their own. Their formula for life is:

I MAKE-------TO HAVE-------TO BE = FULFILLED

FOR EXAMPLE:

I MAKE MONEY-----TO HAVE POSSESSIONS-----TO HELP ME
FULFILL MY POTIENTIAL

= SELF-REALIZATION.

Obviously, we need possessions to get on in life. Whether we have more or less is not the issue here. The question is whether our feelings of self-realization *depend* on having possessions. We don't realize how attached we are to material things until we lose them. Many people suffer severe depression if they lose their source of income. If they identify their self-worth with what they have, they are ready for suicide as soon as they are financially wiped out.

Alternative attitude

The following formula is based on an intuition of one's inherent worth attached to one's being and on the power of creativity to enlarge one's life through the production of beauty:

I AM-------I HAVE-------I MAKE = WORLD-MAKING

I am   =   A realization of ourselves as fully worthwhile simply because we are.

Included in the awareness of "I am" is the awareness of our powers of intuition, self-reflection, creativity and ultimate choice.

Included in the awareness of "I am" is the awareness of the fullness, completeness and perfection of the spiritual dimension of our being.

Included in the awareness of "I am" is the awareness of the kinetic and undrainable source of energy in the spiritual dimension of our being.

I have = A realization of all the psychological and physical powers and talents that are mine, such as the power to communicate in words and symbols, the power to move physically, the power to use ideas, the power to use things.

I make = A realization that we live in the social, moral, economic, political and cultural world that we make.

To make means to transform the ideals that are born of our intuition into practical ways of living.

To make means to transform the possibilities that we see in our creative minds into actualities.

To make means to use our psychological and physical powers to shape ourselves into a unique artistic work inspired by our spiritual powers of intuition and creativity.

To make means to shape a world of human relations inspired by the ideals of love and justice.

To help the skeptic adopt the belief of—I am, I have, I make = world making—we have to show him how to get in touch with his tendency of vision. We can use the same strategies that we used when we described how to help the confused person move to vision. However, we have to keep in mind that for the skeptic these strategies aim at developing a sense of trust in his own intuition. As soon as he makes the ultimate choice to trust his own deepest intuitions of himself and of life, he will experience a sense of peace and power. Then, he can get on with making his world instead of suspecting and fighting it.

Chapter XII

PUTTING IT ALL TOGETHER

Helping is an art. The development of an art requires the improvement of skills, the understanding of theory and continuous reflection on one's performance. All of that sounds so cold and clinical to a person that just wants to be a friend to someone. Many people that want to help others are put off by the use of methods and techniques. They feel that they are being manipulative instead of spontaneous, distant instead of close and superior instead of equal. In this chapter I want to make the point that a true helper and friend is someone that can be *both* close *and* methodically skillful in cooperating with a person asking for our help. I also want to make the point that someone that tries to help another person without bothering to develop skills and method is not much of a helper or friend. Helping is a demanding and self-sacrificing art, if done well. It is done well when we are there primarily for the sake of the other person. We are there to cooperate with him in making *his* world. If we truly care for others, we will put the time and energy into developing skills and understanding theories and methods that will make us useful to people. Making a helping relationship requires attentiveness, exactness, planning and skill. We take these characteristics for granted when making our material world. If we ask the carpenter to make a cabinet, we expect a perfect product. Then, we take care of that cabinet diligently. If one of our children treats the cabinet roughly, do we craft our response with the same attentiveness, planning and skill that the carpenter used. Or, do we "help" our child respect a work of art by flying off the handle? How often do we find ourselves caught up in these contradictions? Is it because we have not learned how to translate our intentions into action? How often have we become angry with our children, parents, spouses and brothers and sisters, "only because we love them"? Anger and the habits of anger never make love. Afterwards, we have

119

to explain away our anger by telling people how much we love them. However, true love is love that is made with diligence, skill, practice, method and understanding as well as with affection. We probably experience frustration more than anger in our helping relationships. Frustration is the emotion that we experience when we believe that we can't achieve our goals. We might want to help someone, but we don't know how. We become frustrated. Then we get angry at ourselves over our frustration. We can avoid all of this by learning how to be more attentive to the movements in other people and by learning a method to be cooperative in helping people move freely and creatively.

Method and Skills

The following chart shows the relationships between our tendencies and the process of life and between our tendencies and the methods and skills that we can use to advance the supra-rational tendencies of the person that we are helping.

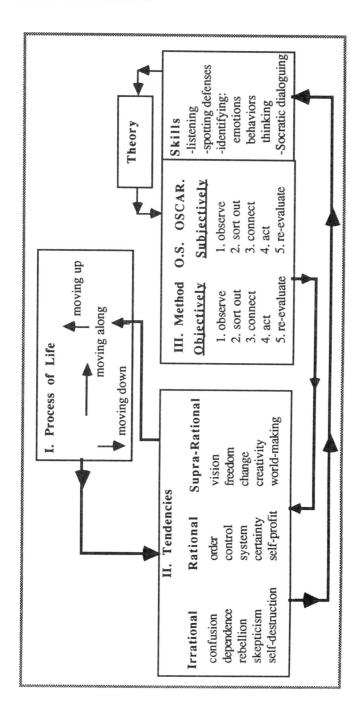

The process of helping starts in Box 1. The helpee feels that he is either moving down or that he is stuck, and he is afraid to move lest he will tumble down all the way. The feeling of moving down could be related to any area of his life: work, relationships, family or feelings about himself. The down feeling might be so strong in one area of his life that it affects his attitude and performance in the other areas, or the down feeling might be relatively confined to one area of his life.

The irrational tendencies in Box II explain his feelings of moving down in Box 1. *The first goal* of the helper is to work with the helpee to develop his awareness of the dominant tendencies that explain his feelings of moving down. *The second goal* of the helper is to cooperate with the helpee in removing all the obstacles, such as irrational thinking and blaming others that prevent him from moving toward his supra-rational tendencies. *The third goal* of the helper is to cooperate with the helpee in connecting his supra-rational tendencies in a practical way to his everyday life so that the helpee feels that he is on his way up toward making his world.

The method and skills in Box III are the resources of the helper. The method and skills in Box III will help the helper achieve his three goals.

Method
Method simply means a step by step process that helps us to accomplish what we have in mind. The acronym **O.S. OSCAR** stands for:

$$O = \text{objectively} \quad S = \text{subjectively}$$

O = observe
S = sort out
C = connect
A = act
R = re-evaluate

The steps in the method are:

1. Objectively observe   2. Subjectively observe
3. Objectively sort out   4. Subjectively sort out
5. Objectively connect   6. Subjectively connect
7. Act
8. Re evaluate

Let's use the following story to show how the method works:

John says he feels really down. At thirty-five he feels he is going nowhere is his career. He hasn't received a promotion in years. His superiors take no notice of his work. He feels that his colleagues take him for granted. He complains that he gets no recognition. He's beginning to doubt his own abilities. His doubts prevent him from making a change. His discontentment at work has even sullied his attitude toward his spouse and children.

Step 1 - Objectively Observe

In this step we use the skills of listening and reflecting the emotions and behaviors of John so that he can objectively see himself and his world of work in us. We act as a psychological mirror for John. We will make statements like, "You feel bad about yourself when your superiors neglect you." With more interaction John will be more accurate in describing "feeling bad about himself." "Feeling bad" might mean depressed, or it might mean frustrated. The objective of the helper is to cooperate with John in developing an accurate and concrete description of his actual world and to identify the gaps and contradictions between his actual world and the world that he desires to make.

Step 2 - Subjectively Observe

In this step we are cooperating with John to observe himself subjectively, that is, to help him become aware of what he is doing to move himself down. The skill of helping him label the emotions, behaviors, thinking, assumptions, expectations and values underlying his self-talk will indicate to him the irrational thinking that is fueling his negative emotions and behaviors. The self-talk analysis will also identify the positive values that are not being actualized. For example, John might value initiative, excellence and creativity in work; however, he assumes that his boss has the same values; he assumes that he needs permission or the go-ahead to be creative; he expects gratitude; he thinks empirically, that is, unless the rewards are immediately given he is not motivated to initiate; consequently, he feels depressed and he withdraws. In this step John will see what he ought to change within himself.

Step 3 - Sort Out

In this step we are helping John sort out his ideal concepts (**ICs**) from his operational concepts (**OCs**). The confusion that John experiences is the result of the conflict between his ideal concepts embodied in his values of excellence, initiative and creativity and his operational concepts of waiting for praise and seeking approval before initiating. His operational concepts, that is, the thoughts that guide his immediate day to day actions, move him in the opposite direction from the road leading to excellence, initiative and creativity. John does not see that the assumptions and expectations underlying his ideal concepts are different from the assumptions and expectations of his operational concepts.

Ideal Concepts of excellence, initiative, creativity

> **Assumption**: risk is involved in creativity and initiative. A personal sense of excellence is more important than objective standards.

> **Expectations**: I can expect some negative criticism and some mistakes in the short run when I attempt to do something new. If I want excellence, I can expect more courage from myself to overcome difficulties.

Operational Concepts of seeking approval and waiting for permission

> **Assumptions**: If I have support and permission to act creatively, I will feel more comfortable and I will perform better.

> **Expectations**: I expect my superiors to accept and support my ideas.

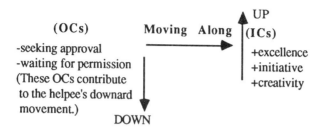

Step 4 - Subjectively Sorting Out

In this step we are helping John sort out his irrational tendencies. If we ask John to identify his emotions, behaviors and thinking when he is seeking approval he will probably say, "I feel anxious. I behave cautiously, tentatively and sometimes awkwardly. I'm thinking about what my boss is thinking. I'm scheming to get his approval." The next step is to ask John to identify the tendency or tendencies on the Human Tendencies Chart that he is experiencing when he uses the operational concept of approval seeking.

Human Tendencies Profile

Irrational	Rational	Supra-Rational
confusion	order	vision
dependence	control	freedom
rebellion	system	change
skepticism	certainty	creativity
(move down toward)	(move toward)	(move up toward)
self-destruction	self-profit	making our world

His emotions, behaviors and thinking connected to the operational concept of approval-seeking combine to form the irrational tendency of dependence. When John does not get approval, he probably experiences the next irrational tendency of rebellion.

The next move is to ask John to recall an experience in his life when he was actualizing his ideal concepts of excellence, initiative and creativity. As he describes the experience, help him label the emotions, behaviors and thinking of that positive experience. He will probably express the emotion of joy, describe his behaviors as alert and adventurous and talk about the excitement attached to the exploration and experimentation of new ideas. Then ask him to identify the tendencies that he was experiencing in the actualization of his ideal concepts. He will probably pick out vision first, and then recite the following supra-rational tendencies on the chart.

At this point John faces a choice. Does he want to continue to move down from dependence to self-destruction, or does he want to move up toward making his world? If he chooses to move up then we can assist him in achieving his goal by first helping him remove the psychological obstacles from his path, such as his operational concept of approval seeking, and then by helping him activate his spiritual powers of self-reflection, intuition, ultimate choice and creativity. We already spoke about the development of these activities in the previous chapters. However, in this step of subjectively sorting out his tendencies, John has to make use of self-reflection, intuition and ultimate choice. But John activated these spiritual powers by getting in touch with past positive experiences. Now, we want to help him use his spiritual and psychological powers to *make* new positive experiences. We are now ready for the next step.

Step 5 - Objectively Connect

In this step we are helping John connect his ideal concepts of excellence, initiative and creativity to his job. To accomplish this objective John needs to create new operational concepts that are consistent with his ideals. By staying in touch with his tendencies of vision and freedom as he looks at his job in the light of his ideal concepts, he will experience the desire to change his negative operational concept of approval seeking. He will also experience his tendency of creativity motivating him to come up with new operational concepts that are in rhythm with his ideal concepts. In this step we are helping John think creatively by exploring different ways of thinking. For example, he could imagine himself as the boss. As a boss what would *he* expect from a creative employee? From this exercise he might see that the operational concepts of communication and persistence are practical and consistent with his ideal concepts. After developing a list of new operational concepts we are ready to move on to the next step.

Step 6 - Subjectively Connect

In this step we are helping John select the operational concepts that suit him best. To do this we will help him foresee the consequences of each operational concept. For example, by listening more attentively to his boss and colleagues what consequences can he expect in terms of understanding them, of knowing when they are ready for a new idea, of establishing a professional atmosphere in which his colleagues and boss will want to know—"What does John think about that"—and of feeling more confident about his own ideas?

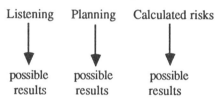

Operational Concepts OCs

Listening   Planning   Calculated risks

possible   possible   possible
results   results   results

Step 7 - Act

In this step we are helping John practice his *operational concept* of listening, so that he develops the *skill* of listening. We might have to demonstrate to him the difference between hearing someone and listening to someone. After he has developed the skill, then he can set goals and objectives for himself. His *goal* might be *to initiate a new idea*. However, he has to convince his boss and colleagues about the merits of his idea. His *objective* might be *to listen* to his boss and colleagues for a set number of specified times over the course of a month before presenting his new idea. Once he has sharpened his skills and refined his plan then he acts.

Step 8 - Re-evaluate

After John has acted he can evaluate his actual consequences against his projected consequences. If the results are not as fruitful as he expected, he can assess his performance, his effort and the appropriateness of the operational concept that he chose. If his effort and performance were not up to the mark, he will have to use a different operational concept or add more OCs to the one he used. If the operational concept "worked," that is, was consistent with his ideal concept, then John will feel that he is moving up. He will also be more in touch with his spiritual powers and his supra-rational tendencies. He will also experience more harmony, order and control in his life. However, as we all know, and, as John will discover, ideal concepts are never realized completely in our lives. Humans are beings on the move toward making themselves and their world better in the light of their ideal concepts. As long as we are on the move upward in our work and relationships, we will feel a sense of joy. The key question to ask in this step is, "Are my thoughts and actions contributing to my upward movement?"

Chapter XIII

DIALOGUING: THE SEED OF VISION

The human tongue is the most dangerous weapon to destroy someone and the most useful tool to help someone. He who does not guard, discipline and develop his language will cause great harm to himself and others. Unless our tongue is connected to our spirit, we will tell ourselves and others lies. When we lie about ourselves, we ultimately do violence to ourselves. When we lie about others, we do violence to them.

Generally speaking, we are very careless in speaking to each other. Compare, for example, the way we use our tongue with the way we use our technological sound and vision systems. We treat our TVs, VCRs and stereos delicately. We learn about them; we fine tune them; we update them. We want the best quality to come out of them. In using our tongues to communicate, do we choose the correct volume and the appropriate pitch? Do we fine tune our vocabulary to use the precise word? Sometimes our speech resembles a stereo being "tuned" by a three-year old. Just as a stereo can be used to produce noise or music, so also our tongue can be used to produce confusion or harmony. How many of us still hear the mindless and nasty criticisms of our parents, our teachers, our colleagues, our bosses, our children, and our friends echoing in our minds? Many people spend a good part of their lives either making their critics eat their own words or getting back at the people that verbally wounded them. Helping people often means undoing the negative feelings and impressions of themselves that were implanted and nurtured by the negative criticism constantly dumped on them by their parents.

As helpers we need to know the art of dialoguing. In dialogue we cooperate with people to discover their inherent value and to clarify their vision of life. Dialogue is the activity of exchanging our intuitions, thoughts, feelings and actions for the purpose of understanding ourselves, each other and life in general. Although we use speech in dialogue, we use it in a special way. The speech that we use in dialogue is the vehicle that moves our spirit into the spirit of another. The speech of dialogue is very different from the speech that we use in other types of exchanges. Let's look at some ways of talking so that we will clearly see the difference between dialogue and these other ways of talking.

Small talk: Using speech to pass the time of day, such as talking about the weather, sports and any other thing that we simply observe and talk about as matters of fact.

Story telling: Using speech to describe an event brought about by actions of people or by nature, such as a car accident, what Johnny did at his fifth birthday party, or the havoc wrought by a hurricane.

Professional or shop talk: Using speech to discuss the activities of a particular career, such as, doctors conferring with each other, or carpenters exchanging working techniques.

"I" talk: Using speech to broadcast one's ego, such as boasting about one's achievement, complaining about one's aches and pains, and whining about one's poor lot in life.

Family talk: Using speech to express our feelings, hopes and responsibilities according to our roles in a family, such as a father encouraging his child, or a daughter asking her mother's advice.

Personal talk: Using speech to express our personal feelings, thoughts and desires to another person that we see as an equal, such as expressing our anxieties about our future to a friend.

There are many other types of talk that we can describe, but the ones that we have listed usually show up in the helping relationship. As we said so many times, helping means cooperating with people that want to move toward living a productive life. They usually want to move from confusion to vision, from their irrational tendencies to their rational and supra-rational tendencies. To achieve our goal as helpers in a helping relationship, we need to use a special type of speech, the speech of dialogue.

In dialoguing we use speech to help people *discover* the reality of themselves. In dialogue we use speech to help people *construct* a vision of life. In dialogue we use speech to help people *choose* a meaning for their lives. In dialogue we use speech to help people *create* a way to live with their vision.

Dialogue is *NOT* telling people how to live. Dialogue is *NOT* a pep talk. Dialogue is *NOT* persuading people. Dialogue is *NOT* preaching to people. Dialogue is *NOT* judging people. Dialogue is *NOT* analyzing people. Dialogue is *NOT* reinforcing positive behavior. Dialogue is *NOT* praising people. Dialogue is *NOT* instructing people.

Let's use the case of a drug user to illustrate the activity of dialoguing:

Helper:	As you have been saying, Jim, you really want to stop your drug habit, but you feel powerless. (Helper is clarifying the conflict between what Jim thinks and wants and what he feels.)
Helpee:	Yeah. When I'm off the stuff, life is so damn hard. I've got problems up to my eyeballs. When I'm busy at work I'm okay. But when I have to face myself, my wife and my little kid, I get scared. I feel so small in front of it all. I just want to get away. As long as I'm high I can get through the day.
Helper:	So, when you have to face yourself, you feel afraid. As you face yourself right now, how do you appear to yourself? (Helper is reflecting Jim's fear and is asking him to use his imagination to visualize himself when he faces himself.)
Helpee:	Small. I feel and look very small to myself.
Helper:	And when you use drugs how do you feel and look to yourself?
Helpee:	Big and free.
Helper:	So, when you use drugs you appear big to yourself, and when you don't use drugs you appear small. Which image, big or small is the *true* reflection of who you are? (The helper is confronting Jim in order to help Jim begin some self-reflection.)
Helpee:	I don't know. As I face myself now, I feel confused. I want to be big and powerful, but I can't seem to be that way on my own. I've always felt less than others...in school, at home. Everyone was better than me. Now, everyone seems to be

more successful than me at work. The strain of trying to keep up with everyone gets to me.

Helper: So you feel confused about yourself, but most of the time you feel small, because you don't feel as successful as your friends and colleagues. (Helper is focusing Jim's attention on the connection between feeling small about himself and feeling unsuccessful.)

Helpee: That's right. I would have it all...money, prestige, a good social life, respect from my wife... if I had the smarts, the talent, I'm just an average guy going nowhere.

Helper: So...you believe that to be a *successful person* and to feel powerful and big, you need money, prestige, a good social life and respect from your wife. Let's look at that belief to see if it really makes sense to you. Suppose for now you and I do not have money or prestige. We sit here together without money and prestige—are we valuable or not valuable? (The helper is helping Jim challenge his belief about what makes a successful person by taking away the attributes of prestige and money. Then, he focuses Jim's attention on the question of whether Jim and himself are valuable. Remember, Jim feels confused. The helper is separating the idea of success from the idea of personal value. Jim seems to be confusing them in his mind.)

Helpee: Well...I guess we are both valuable right now. I mean...everyone is worth something.

Helper (At this point the helper will challenge Jim to discover the reason *why* he believes that they are both valuable, and why everyone is valuable.): So even though we are not rich and are not famous, still we are valuable. *Why* do you believe that we are valuable then?

Helpee: I *feel* that we are valuable.

Helper: You *deeply* feel your own value?

Helpee: Yeah...I feel it. I mean...my value doesn't depend on what I have.

Helper: (At this point the helper wants to reinforce Jim's *intuition* of his personal value. Jim sees that he

is valuable simply because he *is* and not because he has things.): So you see that you are valuable because you are and not because of what you have. When you concentrate on that vision of yourself as valuable, how do you feel?

Helpee: I feel strong...hopeful. I feel that I can do something with my life.

Helper: (The helper will label Jim's experience of himself so that Jim will be able to understand the movement taking place in himself.): So...you feel free?

Helpee: Yeah...that's it, free.

Helper: At this moment you feel free and you see that you are valuable. You have moved yourself from depending on drugs to avoid facing yourself and from depending on money and prestige to feel your own personal value. I feel that as long as you concentrate on your personal vision of yourself, you will feel powerful enough to change the order of your life and to take control of your life.

The purpose of dialogue

In dialogue we use speech and actions to help the helpee activate his powers of intuition, self-reflection, ultimate choice and creativity. True, substantial and lasting movement from irrational tendencies to supra-rational tendencies will take place only if the helpee uses the powers of his spiritual dimension to develop his psychological and physical dimensions.

The steps of dialogue (using the acronym, O.S. OSCAR, explained in Chapter XII)

Step one: The helper helps the helpee *objectively observe* his own world. The helper reflects the emotions, behaviors and thoughts of the helpee. The helper functions as a mirror for the helpee.

Step Two: The helper helps the helpee *subjectively observe* his emotions, behaviors and thoughts. The helper helps the helpee to do some self-reflection by asking questions that will help the helpee look at his assumptions, expectations and values. For example, in the dialogue above the helper asks if we are valuable only if we have money and prestige. In this step the helpee is labeling his false assumptions and his true values.

Step three: The helper helps the helpee *objectively sort out* his ideals, values and personal vision of himself from the thoughts that direct his day to day life. For example, in the dialogue above the helpee sees that he is valuable in himself, but in his day to day actions the ideas of having prestige and comparing himself to others guide his life.

Step four: The helper helps the helpee *subjectively sort out* his tendencies. In the dialogue above the helpee sees what he is doing and thinking when he is dependent on drugs. He also sees what he is doing and thinking when he feels valuable and free. He is sorting out his irrational tendencies from his supra-rational tendencies.

Step five: The helper helps the helpee *objectively connect* his ideals and personal vision of himself to new ways of thinking and acting that will put order in his life. In this step the helper cooperates with the helpee to activate his creative thinking. For example in the dialogue above the helpee discovers that the operational concept of cooperation is more productive than comparing himself to others.

Step six: In this step the helper helps the helpee *subjectively connect* his new operational idea to particular areas of his life, such as career and relationships. The helpee looks at the possible consequences of his new ideas, such as cooperation, and decides whether to use it and when and where to use it.

Step seven: In this step the helper helps the helpee to *act.* This step is really the outcome of the dialogue. The helpee starts to make his world according to his vision by acting. To act effectively and efficiently the helper cooperates with the helpee in constructing goals and step-by-step objectives to achieve his goals.

Step eight: In this step the helper helps the helpee *reevaluate* his new ideas guiding his day to day life. The helpee evaluates the results of applying his new operational concepts. For example, the helpee wants to see if the idea of cooperation is helping him make his world of work and relationships according to his vision of his inherent self-worth. He will want to know if by using the idea of cooperation he is developing his sense of personal worth, freedom and creativity.

What is the difference between dialogue and instruction?

Dialogue is a special form of communication and one that we rarely experience. Most of our conversations with friends and even spouses fall in the other categories of communication, such as story-telling, professional talk and personal talk. When we try to help people close to us, we fall into the trap of *instructing* them. We want to tell them *how* to do something, such as how to get a job, how to change their bad habits and how to be happy. "How to" talk is usually a list of behaviors that we recommend because we know from our experience that they pay off. We can instruct someone to ice skate, sell insurance, bring up children, advance in a career, control stress, and achieve a hundred other outcomes. However, knowing *how* to do something does not mean that we *will* do it. Instruction reaches the physical and psychological dimensions of a human being. If the spiritual dimension is inactive, instruction is not effective. How often have we felt frustrated after clearly and simply instructing someone how to do something for his own good? We felt frustrated because we didn't teach him. In dialogue we reach someone; in instruction we teach someone. Reaching someone moves a person. Teaching does not always move someone.

Differences between instruction and dialogue

Instruction	Dialogue
1. Primarily addresses what and how questions.	1. Primarily addresses why questions.
2. Aims at developing concepts and behaviors.	2. Aims at developing intuition, self-reflection, creativity and choice.
3. Uses examples and models to show people how to do something.	3. Uses socratic dialogue to help people discover their own mind and personal vision of life.

When people dialogue with each other they express themselves from the spiritual center of their being through their psychological and physical dimensions. The following diagram illustrates this movement.

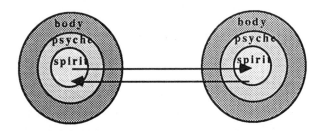

For example if two people are dialoguing about love, then they are expressing their intuitions and personal reflections through the activities of their psyches and bodies. Their concepts and bodily expressions bear the personal and unique imprint of their spiritual insights. They are not simply exchanging ideas that they read in books or heard from someone else. Unfortunately, dialogue is rarely experienced by most of us. If we experienced it more we would need less help in directing our lives.

At this point I find myself in somewhat of a contradiction. I'm giving instructions on how to dialogue just after making the point that dialogue is not instruction. However, we do have to learn by instruction—either formally or informally—how to dialogue even though we have a natural tendency to dialogue. If you follow these instructions and steps mechanically, you will not experience dialogue. These steps and instructions will *facilitate* dialogue. The *human spirit causes dialogue*. To dialogue we must choose to be totally present—spiritually, psychologically and physically—before another person. In dialogue we encounter, that is, we meet each other. We are present and transparent to each other. Also in dialogue we become transparent to ourselves. We require much more than knowledge of the steps and skills of dialogue in order to carry on a dialogue with the person that we are helping.

What is required in order to carry on true dialogue?

Let's use the example of a parent talking with his teenage child about staying out late on Saturday night. Several issues are involved in this particular example: parental authority and responsibility; mutual trust; the teenager's desire for some autonomy; parental anxiety about what can go wrong.

The parent can talk to his teenager as a parent. "This is the rule that I have set. Make sure that you are in the house by nine-thirty."

The parent can take another approach and express his/her personal feelings to his/her teenage child. "You want to stay out until eleven-thirty? Do you realize how much I'll worry about you?"

The parent can take yet another direction. He/she can choose to *dialogue* with his/her teenage child. "You would like to stay out late on Saturday nights. I think that you feel it's important for you to be with your friends." This opening statement starts the conversation on a track leading to what and who are important to the teenager and how he will go about acting out what is important to him. In dialogue the teenager's intuitive sense of value and his self-reflective powers will be activated by his own choice. The teenager will be faced with the challenge of balancing his desire to be with his friends and his desire to be with his parents. The outcome of the dialogue will be an agreed upon time of returning home.

Developing dialogue with teenage children takes time. Laying down the law and demanding absolute obedience is quicker and easier. Giving orders based on our own fears is also quicker. However, neither approach *helps* our teenager to mature. Lasting and effective dialogue requires:

An attentive attitude: An attentive attitude means keeping our eyes on the background of a conversation. An attentive attitude assumes that there is a spiritual depth to each person that ought to be respected. However, not every conversation searches for deep meaning. Talk at times entertains us. Yet, an attentive attitude prepares us to dialogue. An attentive attitude sharpens our judgement to know when and when not to dialogue.

Discipline: Dialogue requires mental and physical discipline. By discipline we mean that we control our thoughts so that they are directed toward the other person. In dialogue we are using our mental abilities to help another person get in touch with and actualize his vision. For example, helping people to spot their defenses and to accept and review their own emotions and thoughts demands that we symbolize our own emotions and direct our own thoughts for the good of the person that we are helping.

Unselfishness: Dialogue is an altruistic activity. In dialogue we concentrate our attention on the other person. Unselfish means to experience oneself moving toward another person for the sake of giving our time, our energy and our minds for the other person. Unselfish does not mean to experience oneself as nothing. On the contrary the unselfish person experiences the fullness of life in giving. When we have given ourselves, then we know how to receive. If we have not given ourselves to someone, it is difficult for us to recognize a person's gift of himself to us.

Patience: We all like to get quick results. In helping people we must remember that we are *cooperating* with them, *not controlling* them. We move at their pace. At times we might behave impatiently, because *we* see clearly the changes that people ought to make. We lose patience when we lose our concentration on what we are doing, namely, to help the other person see.

Belief in the power of the other person: Belief in the power of the person that we are helping follows from our intuitive insight into his spiritual dimension. We believe that he can change his direction, because he has the powers of intuition, self-reflection, ultimate choice and creativity. If our response is motivated by our belief in his resiliency, he will feel the challenge to see himself differently.

What is the difference between exchange and giving freely?

People's relationships today are probably more governed by the idea of exchange than by the idea of giving freely. Using the idea of exchange we judge the quality of friendships, family relationships and romantic love by the balance of payments between the parties. When two people satisfy each other's needs equally well, they believe that they "have" a good relationship. "Having" a good relationship as a personal possession weighs more on the scale of values than the persons in the relationship. Good means that the other person satisfies our needs, and we satisfy his needs. However, the standards that we use to measure satisfaction are very subjective. Relationships based solely on the satisfaction of mutual needs are often nagged by running arguments fueled by wounded pride and unmet expectations. Both parties usually believe that they are satisfying the needs of the other at least according to their own standards. The relationship falls apart because the parties cannot agree on a neutral and objective standard that will guide the behaviors of both.

The idea of control in a relationship flows directly from the idea of exchange. If we believe that a relationship is made up of exchange, then we will believe that we can control the exchange of satisfied needs. Control usually means making the other person dependent on us. For example, we can make sure our partner's need for attention is satisfied by rewarding him or her with an abundance of affection after he or she has satisfied our pressing needs first. Eventually, both parties will become dissatisfied with the game that they are playing.

The relationship that is based on exchange starts off as an **R-R/R** relationship in terms of human tendencies:

R - I will satisfy - **R** - Then I will reciprocate

R- Our relationship is good for the self-interest of both of us.

Because the exchange does not balance equally, the relationship changes to an **I-R/I,**

I - I need your attention to   **R** - I will give you attention

     feel good (dependence).   provided that...(control)

    I - We really cannot trust each other to care for each other unconditionally (skepticism).

The true helping relationship develops on the idea of giving freely. The helper in the helping relationship acts according to his suprarational tendencies of vision, freedom, change and creativity. The helper does not intend to get something out of helping, that is, he does not help to get. He helps to give freely. If the helper *intends* to get something out of the helping relationship, the interaction will turn to an **I-R/I** relationship. The helper will try to control the helpee, and the helpee will become more dependent on the helper. Dialogue cannot take place in this kind of relationship. In any relationship we have to be vigilant so that we avoid the camouflaged traps of our own and other people's irrational tendencies. For example, allowing ourselves to take charge of an irrationally dependent person appears to be a compassionate act. However, common sense tells us that our actions of coming to his rescue reinforces his dependency. Helping, as we said before, means cooperating with another person in the activity of dialogue by which the helpee discovers and actualizes *his* vision of life.

Postscript

THE SUPRA-RATIONAL PERSON

Although we experience the full range of tendencies—irrational, rational, and supra-rational—we choose to make one set dominant in our lives. Some people choose to pay attention to their best intuitions. Others choose to neglect them. Some people choose to open their spirits to the bigness of life. Others choose to close their eyes to any reality that might be bigger than their egos. Those that choose to stay open to their intuitions of Life develop strong supra-rational tendencies.

The supra-rational person is a person of vision that:
- dialogues within himself to explore all the dimensions of his being.
- humbly recognizes that he participates in an infinite reality that he calls Life, God, Being, The One or some other name.
- stays open to new ideas that result from his internal dialogues and his interpersonal dialogues.
- concentrates in order to stay in touch with his best intuitions about himself and others.
- reflects on his ideals from time to time to see where he is and where he is headed.
- looks for possibilities in his own reality and in the reality of others.
- thinks pragmatically in order to actualize the possibilities that he sees.

The supra-rational person is a free person that:
- chooses to take a positive attitude toward Life.

- chooses to participate in the bigness of Life.
- chooses to give more and to take less.
- chooses to distinguish himself as a unique person independent of, but respectful of and attentive to, his sex, culture, race, nationality, religion and immediate family.
- chooses to unite with people simply because they are persons.
- chooses to love intimately without dominating and without possessing.
- chooses to respect the freedom of others.

The supra-rational person is a changing, that is, a developing person that:
- assesses his talents, interests, limitations and possibilities realistically.

- explores real options carefully.

- pursues achievable goals.

- puts out effort to realize his goals.

- is ready to take a risk because he believes in himself and in the power of life.

- is ready to bounce back if he fails.

A supra-rational person is a creative person that:
- trusts his best and deepest intuitions about himself and others.

- looks at himself and others from different angles to find new ways of knowing himself and others.

- thinks fluidly so that his thinking does not become rigid and rusty.

- feels challenged by difficult and complex situations.

- sees each day as a new beginning.

- believes that it is up to him to discover new ways to make his life according to his vision.

The goal of helping means to cooperate with the helpee in strengthening his supra-rational tendencies by warming up his spiritual powers of intuition, self-reflection, ultimate choice and creativity. The successful helper is the person that lives and loves supra-rationally and has learned the art of dialogue.

INDEX

STUDIES IN HEALTH AND HUMAN SERVICES